This book belongs to

_____

a mom after God's own heart.

A Mom After God's Own Heart

Elizabeth George

HARVEST HOUSE PUBLISHERS

EUGENE, OREGON

Cover by Garborg Design Works, Minneapolis, Minnesota

Cover photo © Janie Airey/Digital Vision/Getty Images

A MOM AFTER GOD'S OWN HEART
Copyright © 2005 by Elizabeth George
Published by Harvest House Publishers
Eugene, Oregon 97402
www.harvesthousepublishers.com

Library of Congress Cataloging-in-Publication Data

George, Elizabeth, 1944–
  A mom after God's own heart / Elizabeth George.
      p. cm.
  Includes bibliographical references (p.).
  ISBN-13: 978-0-7369-1572-4
  ISBN-10: 0-7369-1572-9 (pbk.)
  1. Mother and child—Religious aspects—Christianity. 2. Parenting—Religious aspects—Christianity. 3. Child rearing—Religious aspects—Christianity.
  4. Christian education of children. 5. Mothers—Religious life. I. Title.
  BV4529.18.G46 2005
  248.8'431—dc22   2005004646

Printed in the United States of America

05   06   07   08   09   10   11   12   / BP-CF /   10   9   8   7   6   5   4   3   2

Contents

Acknowledgment

As always, thank you to my dear husband, Jim George, M.Div., Th.M., for your able assistance, guidance, suggestions, and loving encouragement on this project. And a special "thank you" for the contribution of your wisdom in the "From a Dad's Heart" sections in this book.

A Word of Welcome

♡

Dear Mom,

Without even meeting you, I can tell you are someone very special! Why? Because you're choosing to read this book. When you consider its title, it becomes pretty obvious that you desire to be a mom after God's own heart. This book is packed with information and how-to's that will show you how to fulfill the desires of your mother-heart—how to become a mom after God's own heart. As we begin our journey together, a few things will make it even sweeter.

Open your book... and enjoy it! Vital information is here. Encouragement is here. God's Word is here. I've even tried to make it easy to read for you as a busy woman and mom. In my mind I've pictured you reading this book in a quiet moment after the kids leave for school...or while the little ones are napping...or as you wait up for your teen to come home...or as you rock your baby to sleep...or maybe even as you recline against a tree while your kids enjoy a romp in the park. Enjoy your book! Carry it with you, and let God's Word instruct you and give you a power boost and a pat on the back all at the same time.

Open your heart... to the priorities and topics covered in this book. They are tailor-made just for you,

7

mom. They'll give you God's wisdom and guidelines for this major role in your life.

Open your heart... through prayer to the Holy Spirit. Ask Him to illuminate God's Word, to help you understand God's plan and priorities for your life, and to transform you, heart and soul.

Open your heart... to others. Look around. Are there other moms in your church or neighborhood who would benefit from learning what being a mom is all about? Invite them to get *A Mom After God's Own Heart* too, and go through it together. Then you'll be growing as moms and in the things of the Lord. And to really accelerate your understanding, go through the *A Mom After God's Own Heart Growth and Study Guide.* You'll love it!

Open your heart... and dream! Dream of becoming the mom you yearn to be—a mom after God's own heart.

And now let's put feet on those dreams! It is the prayer of my heart that the contents of this special book for moms like you will encourage you, excite you, instruct you, and inspire you to follow after God's own heart!

In His great and amazing love,
your friend and fellow mom in Christ,

Elizabeth George

Focusing on the Heart

Focusing on the Heart

Keep your heart with all diligence,
for out of it spring the issues of life.

PROVERBS 4:23

No matter what you do each day...or in life...doing things God's way is a matter of the heart. Whether it's deciding how to spend your money or your time, how you treat people, how you dress, or how you do your work, your choices reveal your heart. And the same is true when it comes to how you raise your children—no matter what their ages.

Why is the condition of the heart—both yours as a mom and the heart of your child—so critical? The Bible answers this all-important question.

At the Heart of All Things

As you already know from personal experience, the heart is the chief organ of physical life. It's obvious to everyone that the heart occupies the most important place in the human system. But the heart, as used in the Bible, also stands for our entire mental and moral activity, including the emotions, the ability to reason, and the will. The heart is also used figuratively for "the hidden springs of the personal life."[1] That's why God warns and instructs us to "keep [our] heart with all diligence, for out of it spring the issues of life" (Proverbs 4:23).

God begins molding a mother after His own heart on the inside— in the inner woman and her heart— and then works outward.

In other words, we are "to present our entire beings to God....[and] the heart is first. It speaks of the inner life, the mind, the thoughts, the motives, the desires. The mind is the fountain from which the actions flow. If the fountain is pure, the stream that flows from it will be pure. As a man thinks, so is he."[2]

So what does this have to do with being a mom? First, we need to know how important our child's heart is. W.E. Vine, giving insights into Matthew 15:19-20, wrote, "human depravity as in the 'heart,' because sin is a principle which has its seat in the center of man's inward life, and then 'defiles' the whole circuit of his action." That's the bad news. But, second (and here comes the good news),

Scripture regards the heart as "the sphere of Divine influence" (Romans 2:15; Acts 15:9).[3]

So here, my fellow mom, is our twofold challenge. To raise (and keep on raising!) a child after God's own heart, we must till the soil of each tender heart and sow the seed of the Word of God while praying fervently for "Divine influence." At the same time, we must devote ourselves to diligently training and to dealing with and disciplining the sin that is a part of every child's life.

But where does all of this mothering, committing, praying, dedicating, dealing with, and disciplining begin? It starts in *your* heart, dear mom!

As moms, our job assignment from God is to raise children after God's own heart—children who seek to follow God and hopefully experience salvation through Jesus Christ. And following-through on God's plan for us is all about our hearts. It's all about fulfilling God's instructions to us. He wants us to focus on giving our heart, soul, mind, strength, and time to influencing and shaping the hearts of our children toward God and His purposes.

Children with a Heart for God

You can probably think of men and women in the Bible who had hearts for God, who followed after Him. But there are also a number of children in the Bible who had hearts for God, ranging all the way from pre-schoolers to pre-teens to young adults. These children loved and served God in a variety of ways. And each one of their stories has lessons for us as moms after God's own heart, no matter what our children's ages.

Samuel—Everyone from toddlers to grandparents alike loves the story of the boy Samuel's response to God's call. (You can read about this part of Samuel's life in 1 Samuel 3:1-21.) It's what we dream of for our own growing children...that they never know what it's like to not love and follow God. That's how I see Samuel. He's the young guy whom most believe at around 12 or 13 years old heard God calling him...and answered.

What made Samuel a child after God's own heart? In 1 Samuel 3 we read that he—

> *heard* God's call...and
>
> *answered* Him. He
>
> *listened* to what God had to say, and he
>
> *responded* to the voice of the Lord, saying, "Here I am!...Speak, for Your servant hears" (verses 4 and 10).

From the heart-actions of the boy Samuel it's apparent that "children (even at a very young age) are able to make significant spiritual commitments and substantial contributions to the work of God."[4]

Where does such a heart come from? Certainly, first and foremost, it comes from God Himself. He is the Maker and Creator of all good things, including a heart that hears, listens, answers, and responds to Him. But on the heels of this right response we might also add "...and from Samuel's mother." Who was she? Her name was Hannah, and she was the woman who prayed to God and vowed,

O LORD of hosts, if You will...give Your maidservant a male child, then I will give him to the LORD all the days of his life (1 Samuel 1:11).

The answer to this prayer from Hannah's heart was Samuel...who was dedicated to the Lord before he was even conceived! And to fulfill her vow, Hannah took Samuel to the house of the Lord in Shiloh when he was weaned, at about age three. And there she handed her little tyke over to Eli, God's priest, to be raised under his direct superinten- dence and instruction in the shadow of the house of the Lord.

A mother's greatest joy in having a child is to give that child fully and freely to God.

By age three it appears little Samuel was well on his way to becoming a child after God's own heart. From that tender age he "ministered to the LORD before Eli the priest" (1 Samuel 2:11). And where did such a heart begin to take shape? Again it all began in the plan of God. But another factor in God's plan was the faithful- ness of a mother after God's own heart. Imagine...a mom who could pray the prayer Hannah prayed in 1 Samuel 2:1-10! (Be sure to read it for yourself.)

Imagine her fervent love for God, her knowledge of God through the Pentateuch (the first five books in the Bible) and from His dealings with His people throughout history. Imagine her intense instruction to her little one and her passionate prayers on his behalf as she prepared to deposit her preschooler in Shiloh.

I pray that such a burning dedication to God—and to teaching and training our children—is true of you...and me too.

David—David was the original man after God's own heart (1 Samuel 13:14). But he was also a boy after God's own heart. Scholars believe David was between 10 and 16 years old when Samuel, who grew up to be a prophet and priest, anointed David to be king over Judah.[5] David was brought up to be a shepherd. And there on the slopes of Judah's rolling hills, David, already a lover of the Lord, tended his father's sheep, wrote prayers to God, and sang them to the Lord while playing on his stringed instrument. When concluding a study of David's life, one scholar wrote in a homily entitled *God's Love for Little Boys,* "It is impossible to overestimate the great things which become possible when a young life is surrendered to Almighty God."[6]

And where did such a soft heart for God in a little boy come from? Of course, it began in the sovereign plan of God. But look also at David's spiritual family tree:

Salmon [who married Rahab] begot Boaz, and

Boaz [who married Ruth] begot Obed;

Obed begot Jesse, and

Jesse begot David (Ruth 4:21-22).

These men and women, husbands and wives, mothers and fathers, and grandmothers and grandfathers were filled with faith and used by God. The Bible doesn't tell us much about David's mother and father, but it does tell us about David's lineage and his love for God at a young age...and his knowledge of God had to come from some faithful, obedient sources.

> *God works through faithful parents who, in spite of dark and difficult days, walk obediently with Him.*

Are you a mom after God's own heart, ready and desirous to be used by God in your children's lives? Then ask God to help you faithfully pass on your faith and trust in God from generation to generation so your little ones might be boys and girls and young men and women after God's own heart. Make it the regular prayer of your heart.

Daniel and his friends—Everyone also loves the incredible tales of Daniel and his three friends—Shadrach, Meshach, and Abed-nego (see Daniel 1–3). These young men—the best of the best—were carried away as captives to Babylon by King Nebuchadnezzar. There they were selected for careful training for the king's service. I say "the best of the best" because to be prepared for royal governmental service these youths had to be handsome, physically perfect, mentally sharp, and socially poised and polished (Daniel 1:4). But did you know that many scholars believe that when the book of Daniel opens, these four friends are teenagers, "children...about fourteen or fifteen years of age"[7] or between 14 and 17?[8]

And who were the parents of Daniel and his friends? No one knows for sure. But here's what we do know. This band of four captives was "of the children of Israel" (verse 3): They were descendants of the patriarch Jacob (also known as Israel). They were also "of the king's descendants" (verse 3). In other words, they were of the family of David. And they were "children of Judah" (verse 6), the most noble tribe of Israel. But whoever their parents were, the actions and choices these young men made shout out a loud testimony and build a strong case that their parental training was extremely strong and godly. In their teen years, when so many youths are tempted to question or turn away from their upbringing, these adolescents did the opposite. In fact, they were willing to make God-honoring decisions and stand up for their faith...even if it meant death.

> *From a godly home life and upbringing, a child can learn how to live a godly life in a sinful world.*

Now, imagine *your* child at age 14 to 17, being separated from you and having to make such hard choices. What do you think your teen would choose? Or if your child is younger, what do you hope and pray he or she would choose?

Are you getting it, dear mom? (I know I am!) As moms after God's own heart, we must teach, train, and counsel our children every chance we get. God's truth must be imparted. And we need to pray, pray, pray for God to write our faithful teaching of His Word on the tablet of our children's hearts (Proverbs 3:3). For who knows—like Daniel and Company—what hard times and choices will arise for our beloved children?

Timothy—Here's another young man after God's own heart. Most likely in his late teens or early twenties,[9] Timothy was referred to by the apostle Paul as "a true son in the faith" (1 Timothy 1:2). This young man, in time, became Paul's disciple and right-hand man.

How did this happen? And who was Timothy anyway? Here's what we know about his family.

- ♥ *Timothy's father* was a Gentile and "a Greek" (Acts 16:1) and not a believer in Jesus Christ.

- ♥ *Timothy's grandmother, Lois,* was a Jewess who knew and understood the Old Testament well enough to respond to the gospel of Christ when Paul and Barnabas came into her town (Acts 14:6-7,21-22).

- ♥ *Timothy's mother, Eunice,* was "a Jewish woman who believed" (Acts 16:1) and joined her mother Lois in embracing Christ as her Savior.

♡   *Of Eunice and Lois,* Paul wrote to Timothy, "I call to remembrance the genuine faith that is in you, which dwelt first in your grandmother Lois and your mother Eunice, and I am persuaded is in you also" (2 Timothy 1:5).

So how does a Timothy come about? From what furnace is such a godly young man forged? Certainly and foremost, from God. And, additionally, from the hearts and prayers of godly relatives. In Timothy's case, it was two godly female relatives—a devout mother and grandmother. Even though his father was not a believer in Christ, God provided the boy Timothy with a faithful female spiritual tag-team. And they provided the seed and cultivated the soil where his faith in Christ could take root and bloom and grow.

Do you need encouragement? Take these words to heart—"Despite division within the home, Timothy's mother instilled in him a character of faithfulness that carried into adulthood....Don't hide your light at home: Our families are fertile fields for receiving gospel seeds. It is the most difficult land to work, but it yields the greatest harvests. Let your [children]...know of your faith in Jesus."[10]

Mary—Here's a young woman after God's own heart. Mary, the mother of our Lord, was only about 14 years old when she "found favor with God" (Luke 1:30). She was chosen to be the human vessel for physically bringing the Son of Man into the world. Was she a woman of nobility, wealth, or education? No. Was she married to someone important? No. In fact, she wasn't married at all.

Well, what was she then? What qualified Mary to be so blessed and honored...and trusted...by God? It was the focus of her heart. You see, Mary was a woman—albeit a young one—after God's own heart. We hear Mary's heart for God in these two instances:

> *Mary's response to God*—When told the mysterious thing that was about to happen to her—about the details of Jesus' birth—Mary replied, "Behold the maidservant of the Lord! Let it be to me according to your word" (Luke 1:38).

> *Mary's response in praise*—Mary's son Jesus said, "Out of the abundance of the heart the mouth speaks" (Matthew 12:34). And that's exactly what we hear in "Mary's Magnificat" or canticle (Luke 1:46-55). Out of her tender young heart tumbled God's own Word. Drawing from the words of the prayers, the law, the psalms, and the prophets of the Bible, which Mary knew by heart, her lips leaked her heart's content. Her heart, soul, and mind were saturated with God's truth.

The role of godly parents is to make sure the hearts and minds of their children are saturated with the Word of God.

How could this be? How can such a thing happen to—and be true of—a mere teenage girl? We know it was God's doing...and God's choice. He, the Sovereign One, found favor in and graced the young Mary and blessed her among women (Luke 1:42).

And who were her parents? We don't know. But we do know culturally that as a female, Mary was taught, encouraged, instructed, and educated in the Scriptures mostly at home. *Someone* at home made sure Mary knew about God.

Are you inspired? Encouraged? Thirsty to live out God's plan for you as a mom? Doing things God's way is always a matter of the heart. That includes choosing to focus your heart on raising your children God's way and praying with each breath that they will develop hearts after God.

Dear mom, no matter what your situation at home is— whether your children believe in Jesus Christ or not, whether they are young or older, whether their dad is a Christian or not (whether there is a dad or not!), whether you are new in the faith or know a lot, whether years of ignorance or neglect of God's Word have gone by up to this point—do your best. From this second on, give your best efforts.

And since you want your children to love God and follow Him, set the focus of your heart on God and let them see you love Him and follow Him. Just be a mom after God's own heart. He'll help you take care of everything else that goes with parenting.

From a Dad's Heart

Hi, this is Jim George, Elizabeth's husband and the father of our two grown daughters, who are now in the throes of trying to raise their seven little ones to be children after God's own heart. Throughout this book I'll be picking up my pen to add my thoughts and advice about what it means to be a mom after God's own heart who is seeking to raise children with a heart for God. My goal is...

♡ to encourage you in your efforts. Christian parenting is hard work! But keep in mind that you are fulfilling one of God's highest callings upon your life—to raise your children to love and serve Jesus Christ.

♡ to provide a dad's and husband's perspective on this serious matter of training up children for God's purposes. Your husband may or may not be vitally involved in this day-in, day-out process. Or he may be a man whose job takes him away from home more than either of you likes (as was the case for Elizabeth and me). And your husband is probably a very busy man as he provides financially for you and the kids.

Each of these reality scenarios puts added pressure on you. But hopefully I will be bringing you fresh insights on the importance of your role and responsibilities as a mom. I'll also be offering you some help along the lines of communicating with your husband about family matters. I'll present tips and principles that will benefit you as a parent. And, if your husband is interested in what you are doing and reading, you can share this section—or any part of this book, for that matter—with him.

As you know, parenting is a challenge. But everything of value is that way, and no one and no pursuit should be more important to you than your family—except God. So remember the apostle Paul's words to your heart...

Be steadfast, immovable, always abounding in the work of the Lord, knowing that your labor is not in vain in the Lord (1 Corinthians 15:58).

Whatever effort, hardships, sacrifices, or inconveniences being a parent requires of you, your hard work is *never* in vain in the Lord.

Now prayerfully consider Elizabeth's "Little Choices that Reap Big Blessings"—choices that will help you be the mom after God's heart you desire to be.

Little Choices That Reap Big Blessings

1. Develop a template for your weeks.

What does your average week look like? What patterns do your days fall into? And what do you want your week to look like? Or what must your week look like to accomplish (with God's help) the raising of children with a heart for God? A week is a fairly little increment of your life. But because it's repeated again and again, it's a mighty thing.

Fine-tune what's already going on in your home so you are truly putting first things first. Mastermind a schedule that allows time for both you and your children to have a daily Bible or Bible-story time (depending on their ages).

Also plan in time for getting ready to go to church (clothes, Bibles, any preparations) so no one is stressed out by the time you all get there. Then plan your church day. Fill it with loads of fun, and of course, like a good mom, plan lots of food!

2. Analyze your TV time.

(And this goes for your kids' TV time too.) Do you know exactly how much time you, "a mom after

God's own heart" (and your "children after God's own heart"), are watching TV? Chart or record it for a while if you like. Then think about how you could use that time to grow in your knowledge of God, to put better things into your heart and mind, to pray for your family to follow God.

How did the young woman Mary come to know the scriptures that became the heart of her prayer of praise? How did Hannah manage to pour life-changing religious teaching into her little boy before he was three years old? How did the young lad David find the time to meditate on God's nature, write his worshipful poetry, and offer it up to God in song? We know the obvious answers, don't we? (And it has nothing to do with TV—and everything to do with time!) These acts of devotion occurred because there was *time* for them to occur. There was also a passionate heart-desire to see them occur. These faithful believers were fiercely intent on knowing God.

Dear mom, with the TV off (or at least on less), these activities that shape both heart and soul—of both mother and child—are more likely to happen.

3. Choose a devotional book.

A mom after God's own heart feeds her soul, but she's also intent on feeding the souls of her children. Select a devotional book for yourself, and one that's age-appropriate for each child. Then set aside a special time each day for enjoying these books. They will soon become treasures. If your children can read, have them read their books to you. If your children are older, have them tell you what they're learning. And be sure you share how you're growing too. Lead the way to God's heart!

4. Memorize one verse.

Hannah knew God's Word. Mary knew God's Word. Daniel and his friends knew God's Word. Timothy's mother and grandmother (and Timothy too) knew God's Word. And David sang God's Word. (Are you noting the common denominator in these moms and children after God's own heart?) Choose a verse to memorize this week. Don't know where to begin? Then memorize Luke 10:27, Acts 13:22, or Colossians 3:2. Each one is a verse about the heart.

And pick verses for your children. Again, be sure they are age-appropriate. Even an 18-month-old can remember "God is love" (1 John 4:8) and "Be kind to one another" (Ephesians 4:32). Then see how creative you can be at celebrating each verse learned by heart. What fun!

5. Pray for your heart.

Being a mom after God's own heart and raising children after God's own heart is "a matter of the heart"—*your* heart. So pray, dear one, for your heart. Give it to God. And give it to Him each fresh new morning as it arrives with fresh new challenges. Open your heart up fully to Him. Dedicate it to God (Luke 10:27). Cleanse and purify it through prayer (James 4:8). Then pray from the heart for your dear precious offspring as only you, their mom, can.

TRAINING CHILDREN FOR GOD... AND FOR LIFE

Ten Ways to Love Your Children

1

Take Time to Nurture Your Heart

And these words
which I command you today
shall be in your heart.

DEUTERONOMY 6:6

God has blessed Jim and me with two wonderful daughters—Katherine and Courtney—who, to date, have been married 10
and 11 years respectively. And now they are seeking to
be moms after God's own heart to the seven little ones
they have between them. As they continually tell me,
"Mom, it's payback time. For everything we dished out to
you, we're getting it right back!"

When Courtney was expecting one of her children,
our church in Washington hosted a baby shower for her,
and our pastor's wife asked me to share a devotional
during the party. It was then, when I sat down to prepare

something for the shower talk, that I wrote out a brief bare-bones list I entitled "Ten Ways to Love Your Children." Believe me, it was a soul-searching exercise to go cover to cover through my Bible and look back at my own attempts at child-raising. And it was a lot of fun at the shower to pass my list on to the other mothers and grandmothers, who were at every age and stage in the parenting process.

Then several years later, my list of ten child-raising principles made its way into one of my books as I wrote about being a mom in a particular chapter.[1] And in time, as I began to speak and share these parenting practices and interact with more and more moms and grandmoms, God planted a desire in my heart to expand them into a book to (I hope and pray!) help moms like you.

So here they are—ten ways to be a mom after God's own heart, also known as "Ten Ways to Love Your Children." As we go along, I want to ask you to do three things. First, please pray. And second, please open your heart to the scriptures presented in this book. They are God's instruction for mothers—from His heart to ours. Third, if you want to know more about being a mom after God's own heart, the additional questions in the Growth and Study Guide book[2] will take you through even more of what God has to say on this vital subject.

> Prayer is the only way of becoming the mom God wants you to be.

Dear reader, the Holy Spirit will use and empower God's Word to teach you and transform you into a mom after God's own heart. After all, your heart is where raising a child after God's own heart begins. So obviously, the first way to love your children is to take time to nurture your heart.

It's All About Your Heart

Imagine this scene. God's people have at last arrived at the borders of the Promised Land, "a land flowing with milk and honey" (Deuteronomy 6:3). They are gathered together for a time of preparation and instruction before crossing the Jordan River to enter their new homeland. It was then and there that their faithful leader Moses gave them a second recitation and review of the law of God.

At the core of Moses' heart was a concern for the generations to come—generations who were not present when God initially gave His law to His people. Moses knew it was critical that those present pass on their knowledge of God's law and the history of His dealings with the Israelites to their children. Hear now Moses' words—and his heart—from Deuteronomy 6:4-12. They contain major instructions to us as parents today.

> 4 Hear, O Israel: The LORD our God, the LORD is one!
>
> 5 You shall love the LORD your God with all your heart, with all your soul, and with all your strength.

6 And these words which I command you
today shall be in your heart.

7 You shall teach them diligently to your children, and shall talk of them when you sit in
your house, when you walk by the way,
when you lie down, and when you rise up.

8 You shall bind them as a sign on your
hand, and they shall be as frontlets between
your eyes.

9 You shall write them on the doorposts of
your house and on your gates.

12 ...lest you forget the LORD.

Did you notice how many times God used the words
"you" and "your" in these verses that make up a call from
God to a total commitment to Him? Be sure and count
them for yourself, but after several tries, I came up with
21 times. Twenty-one! These repeated personal pronouns
make it obvious that God's message to your heart is that
you are to center your life on the Lord. In other words,
being a woman—and a mom—after God's own heart is
all about *you* and *your heart*. (I hope this is sounding a
little familiar!)

A quick walk-through of these verses reveals what
God has in mind for His moms...and for you.

Verse 4—"Hear, O Israel: The LORD our God, the LORD
is one!" These words began the *Shema,* the Jewish "con-
fession of faith" in the one and only true God. "It is the
heart principle of all the covenant stipulations."[3] Today—

as it was then—there are those who put their trust in different "gods." Exactly where is your trust? Your heart? Your commitment? I hope it's to the God of the Bible!

Verse 5—"You shall love the LORD your God." Here God calls you to love Him with an unreserved, whole-hearted commitment of love, a love that includes *"all* your heart...*all* your soul and...*all* your strength." This love is to be an entire, all-consuming "sacred fire"[4] that causes all of your life to reach toward God.

Verse 6—Why is it important that "these words" that make up a part of the law of God be in a mother's heart? Because God knows that when His Word and teachings reside in a person's heart, that person can then think upon them, meditate on them, understand them...and obey them, which is the end-result desired of every person (and mom!) after God's own heart.

Verse 7—Once God's Word and instructions are in your heart, you can then pass them on and "teach them diligently to your children." You can place God and His Scriptures at the heart of the conversations in your home and throughout each day as you "talk of them when you sit in your house, when you walk by the way, when you lie down, and when you rise up."

Verse 8—The instruction of this verse is saying that it's good to be actively meditating on the commandments of God at all times. You can never forget or get away from something that is as near to you as a "sign on your hand" and "between your eyes."

Verse 9—You are to do whatever it takes to make the Scriptures familiar to your heart and to your children... even if it means you "write them on the doorposts of your house and on your gates."

Verse 12—Why all of this attention to having your heart filled with God's instructions and purposefully passing it on to your children? God said through Moses it is "lest you forget the LORD." God forbid that we or our children—our "heritage from the LORD" and His "reward" (Psalm 127:3)—should forget the Lord! God's Word in your heart will keep you from forgetting God—from forgetting your dependence upon Him, from forgetting your need of Him, and from forgetting your obligations to Him and to your children.

Taking Care of Business

Dear mom, are you hearing God's message? Before we can even get to mothering and training our dear precious children, we need to take care of business with God. We need to take care of our own hearts. We need to take time to nurture our hearts. You see, *we* are to love the Lord. And *we* are to love and obey His Word. His Word is to reside in *our* hearts. It really is all about us as moms and our hearts.

And what will happen (by God's grace) if our hearts are dedicated to God? What will happen if our hearts are filled with love for the Lord and with His instruction? We will be godly mothers. And then...*then!*...we can more successfully teach God's Word to our children. Complete devotion to the Lord must first be in the heart of the mother—in your heart and my heart. And then our godly training of our children and our diligent teaching of God's Word will follow.

I like the way one scholar summed up Deuteronomy 6:4-9 for us: "We are to love God, think constantly about his com-

> *The prerequisite for teaching your children about God successfully is that you love God completely.*

mandments, teach his commandments to our children, and live each day by the guidelines in his Word."[5]

Let the Transformation Begin!

My girls are 13 months apart, which means that during their at-home years, I often felt like I had twins! So I had to really be on my toes because there would be little-or-no catching of the mistakes I made on the first child so they weren't repeated on the second one. What I was—or wasn't—doing to love and raise my children was being done to both of them at the same time.

So early on I realized the importance of getting God's powerful Word into my heart each day. I tasted the powerful effect it had on my parenting and on the atmosphere in our home. And the same is true for you. What happens to us moms when we don't take time to nurture our hearts? Here's my list. I found myself...

...running on empty. And when we're spiritually running on empty, our hearts are hollow and numb. Without spiritual refueling, our parenting is empty and the evidences of our apathy creep into our children's lives. All becomes dull and devoid of spiritual energy, purpose, motivation, and accomplishment in both parent and child.

...heartless. If we are heartless, our parenting becomes heartless and rote. We unconsciously put ourselves and our child-raising on autopilot. We find ourselves giving in and giving up the fight for godly standards and behavior. We begin putting up with things the way they are. We fail to make the effort to see that we live out God's calling to be moms after Him. We fail to make sure our children's hearts are being continually molded heavenward.

...worldly. If we are preoccupied with the things of this world and enamored by earthly pursuits and rewards, our parenting will be worldly. We won't be following God's criteria and God's ways. We'll be walking and parenting in the ways of the world. We'll slip up on holding the line on conduct and choices and discipline. The things of this world will creep into our homes and into our children's hearts.

...carnal or unspiritual. If we are fulfilling the lust of the flesh instead of walking in the Spirit (Galatians 5:16), our parenting will show it. As Paul points out, "the works of the flesh are *evident*" (verse 19). There will be screaming, yelling, belittling, name-calling, maybe even the slapping or shaking or pushing of children around.

This is all serious stuff...all brought about because the goodness of God's Word is not regularly refreshing and reminding us of Christ's better ways. God's solution? Pick up the Bible and read it. When we do, God touches and transforms our hearts into those of moms after His heart.

Strength for Each Stretching Day

Recently my Courtney had Baby #4, our beautiful little Grace. Jim and I were there at Courtney's home in Connecticut on baby-watch duty when she and Paul left in the middle of the night for the hospital. We stayed about ten days afterward to help out and ease the usual adjustments of a busy household to a new baby.

I carry one very special memory with me... Each day at breakfast Courtney sat and ate with (and tended to) her five-, four-, and two-year-olds, and Jim and me. (In case it hasn't sunk in yet, that's six people for breakfast...not to mention a baby in a bassinet!) Beside her place mat was her beat-up, well-worn *One Year Bible*.[6] And later, after the dishes were cleared away, the kitchen cleaned up, faces and hands wiped, and the little ones sent on to their next activities, Courtney sat down again at the breakfast table, by herself, with a large glass of water...and read her Bible.

Now I ask you, how does a mom handle each stretching day? How does she manage, in a God-pleasing way, her marriage, her housework, the first baby, the second baby, the third baby, and the fourth baby...all of whom quickly become active toddlers and preschoolers? Answer: She looks to God's empowering—and peace-producing!—Word. And doing so makes a difference—a huge difference!

> *The degree of our spiritual strength will be in direct proportion to the time we spend in God's Word.*

I don't know how other mothers manage to fit in their daily Bible time, but this is how one mom does it as near to every day as she can. It's a powerful habit every mom can build into her life.

Heart Response

What does it take to read through the *One Year Bible*—or any Bible? It takes about 10 to 12 minutes a day. That's roughly the same time as a quick internet session. That's one-half of a good conversation on the phone with your sister, mom, or best friend. That's one-third of a sitcom on TV. That's one-sixth of a television talk show.

But with an earnest, hungry heart, you rise up from those dozen minutes in the Word filled. You are enthused (from *entheos,* meaning *inspired in* or *from God*) instead of heartless and apathetic. You have set aside worldliness and instead set your mind and heart on things above "where Christ is, sitting at the right hand of God...not on things on the earth" (Colossians 3:1-2). And God's spiritual "fruit of the Spirit"—His "love, joy, peace, longsuffering, kindness, goodness, faithfulness, gentleness, self-control" (Galatians 5:22-23)—is evident.

For top performance, refuel daily from God's Word.

Remember, God's Word makes all the difference in the world in your heart, in your day, and in your parenting. This handful of minutes is such a tiny investment to make in something that produces such massive daily—and eternal—dividends!

The excellent and godly mother in Proverbs 31:10-31 rose up each day to tend to the fire of the house (verse 15)...and to the "sacred fire" of her heart (verse 30). Won't you do the same? It's a little choice that will reap big benefits...both in your heart and in the hearts of your children. It will accelerate you down the path to being a more dedicated mother after God's own heart.

From a Dad's Heart

I think you can see the foundational importance of this chapter when it comes to being a mom after God's own heart. You cannot effectively impart to your children what you do not possess yourself. And what better possession is there to pass on to your children than your own heart and passion for God?

And you can make a difference even if your husband isn't a Christian! No matter how little support you receive from him, you can still mark your children for life and eternity. Why can I confidently say this? Because my mother did just that in my life. My father was not a Christian, nor was he interested in spiritual things. But my mother faithfully instilled God's principles into my life.

I can still picture my mom with her open Bible on the kitchen table. Each day she would sit down for a few minutes between her duties and read, study, and pray. And she always talked to me about what she was reading, even up until our last talk here on earth several years ago. She also read Bible stories to me when I was a little boy underfoot. It was during one of these casual talk-times that she introduced me to Jesus Christ as Savior. She took me to church several times a week. It wasn't easy, but she passed on to me what was most precious to her—a love for Jesus.

If you are reading this book and, like my mother, are having to do most, if not all, of the spiritual training of your children by yourself, don't be discouraged. And also don't use your difficult situation as an excuse. Raising your children is too important an assignment from God. Make sure you are growing spiritually yourself, so that you can be a spiritual model for your children.

Or, if you are reading along and your husband is involved in the spiritual training of your children, be sure you don't let or expect him to do it all. Your children need not only a dad after God's own heart, but they also need a mom after God's own heart. You can never give your kids too much spiritual input. Let them know how important God is to you.

My life is a living testimony to a mom who took the time to nurture her heart. And with an abundant love for Jesus overflowing from her heart, she nurtured my heart, so that today and any day I have an opportunity, I rise up and call her blessed (Proverbs 31:28).

*Little Choices
That Reap
Big Blessings*

1. Read your Bible every day.

When you do, you'll hear God's voice and His personal and direct instructions to you. The Bible is the ultimate book on parenting, and as you look to it for help, you'll find the words of Isaiah 30:21 to be true: "This is the way, walk in it." God's Word will guide you each step of the way through each day.

Is your husband gone a lot (or unreachable when a crisis occurs)? Or is he by choice uninvolved in the Child-Raising Department? Or too busy? Every mother experiences one—or all—of these scenarios at some time in her mothering career. But when they occur, God's sure, faithful, error-proof Word of instruction is always there to help you know exactly what to do. Just read it—even for ten minutes a day—and your knowledge will multiply so rapidly you'll surprise yourself by how quickly and thoroughly you learn to handle mothering God's way!

(To help you with this little choice that reaps the biggest of all blessings, I've included a "Quiet Times Calendar" in the back of your book for marking the days you read your Bible. You'll be encouraged as you look it over and see all the boxes you've marked.)

2. Learn from the parents in the Bible.

As you read your Bible, you'll find examples of parents and parenting methods—both good (for instance, Hannah and Mary and Joseph) and bad (Eli and Isaac and Rebekah). Through them you can learn what to do...and what not to do...as a mom and a parent. Try to jot down what you are learning in the form of a principle. (For example, regarding Isaac and Rebekah, the principle could be simply stated, "Never show favoritism.") These biblical principles will guide you through the years.

3. Start saying *no.*

God's Word empowers you when you read it and gives you the strength you need to be a loving-but-firm parent. It's tough to stand up to pressure and say *no* to the world, to others, to your child. It's also hard to say *no* to yourself and your flesh and get up early, stay up late, and go into action in the middle of the night when there's a need (all of which are required of a mom!). That's when strength is absolutely necessary—spiritual, mental, emotional, and physical strength.

Dear faithful mom, God's strength comes to your rescue at just such times to energize you to follow-through on whatever you must do to follow His will. All of your parenting will benefit from the strength you draw from God to say *no* to what does not honor Him or benefit your children.

4. Cherish the good times.

Faithful parenting is challenging work. But it is truly a "labor of love" and certainly a choice that reaps the greatest blessings of all to a mom's heart.

And I admit, sometimes it seems like you'll never get a break, that you'll never make it, that you're going to lose it, that there is no hope and no end in sight, that things seem to be getting worse instead of better. That's why you need to take notice of those peaceful, idyllic pockets and moments of joy and goodness that happen along during your days. You know, those times when all things are well, when things are going the way you—and the Lord—want them to go, when the children are charming, delightful, cheerful, and loving.

Thank God profusely for these good times. Cherish them in your heart-of-hearts. Enjoy them to the hilt. And remember them forever by recording them in a special notebook, album, or memory book. Doing so will give you something to return to over and over again when you need to see some light and remember some good times. Remembering the good times will keep you going for days on end when you are tempted to wonder if being a mom is worth the struggle. Recalling them will turn your heart into a fountain of joy...which, in turn, will refresh your days and your commitment to God's job assignment to you to "train up" your children for Him.

5. Refuse to give up.

Burn this "little choice" into your heart, mind, and muscles! Even when there's no one else—no husband, mother or mother-in-law, sisters, support group, friends, or mentors—to help you or tell you that you are doing the right thing, that you are doing a good job, God shouts forth His "Well done, good and faithful mom" through His Word (Matthew 25:21). When you take time to nurture your heart in God's Word, you receive—directly from God!—the encouragement you need to keep on keeping on in your parenting.

2

$\mathcal{T}$each Your Children God's Word

*And these words
which I command you today
shall be in your heart.
You shall teach them diligently
to your children.*

DEUTERONOMY 6:6-7

h, the joy of having a baby! At last, someone to love, to sing lullabies to, to share nursery songs and rhymes with, someone to whom you want to teach everything you know. And what a thrill it is to one day hear a little voice singing, reciting, and reading to you!

I grew up with two brilliant and dedicated schoolteachers as parents. My dad taught vocational education, and my mother was an English teacher. She was a great and enthusiastic mom, especially when it came to reading to her children. She read...and read...and read(!) to me and my three brothers. And throughout the day she was

51

forever bursting forth with some part of a memorized poem or rhyme. So you can probably guess what I began doing when I became a mom of two little girls. I started reading Mother Goose to them and singing classic little children's songs to and with them.

The Starting Point for a Mom After God's Heart

Then, miracle of miracles, by God's great grace, I became a Christian! After 28 years of floundering in my personal life and trying everything that came down the pike (whether it was the fad-of-the-day, philosophy, psychology, Eastern religions, or self-realization), I heard the gospel of Jesus Christ...and God graciously opened my heart to believe in Him.

In the split-second it took me to think-pray-respond-and-say, "Hey, I believe this!" I was a new creature in Christ (2 Corinthians 5:17). I was born again (John 3:3)! God gave me a new heart and a new life, the kind only He can give! And that split-second of placing my trust— and heart and life—in Jesus was the beginning, the starting point, of every mom after God's own heart, including you, dear reading mom.

And my life changed as God began His transforming work...which meant things changed for my children too. First of all, I purchased a Bible. And I dove into it and devoured it! I was starving to death...and oh-so-thirsty! My life until then had been helpless, hopeless, and purposeless. And God came to my rescue and put me on sure footing. I felt like David must have when he wrote that God "brought me up out of a horrible pit, out of the miry clay, and set my feet upon a rock, and established my steps" (Psalm 40:2). So I read...and I read...and I read my new Bible—over and over and year after year. I marked in it. I memorized parts of it. And I studied through it.

A second thing that happened to me as a new "mom after God's heart" was I began to teach my little ones about God too. That's because of Deuteronomy 6:4-12. This passage marked my mothering for life! We spent the previous chapter on these verses, but for our purposes here, I want to point us specifically to verse seven:

> *The soul of a child is the loveliest flower that grows in the garden of God.* [1]

You shall teach them diligently to your children, and shall talk of them when you sit in your house, when you walk by the way, when you lie down, and when you rise up.

Through this verse God spoke to my heart about my children's hearts. Through it He gave me my job assignment as a mom after His own heart—He wanted me to be a *teacher* after His heart too! And His message is to you as well. From Deuteronomy 6:7 we learn...

—*Who* is to teach? Every believing parent.

—*Who* are you to teach? Your children.

—*What* are you to teach? God's Word.

—*How* are you to teach? Diligently.

—*When* are you to teach? All day long, every day.

—*Where* are you to teach? At home and everywhere.

As we look at training your children for God and at the importance of teaching God's Word to your children, hopefully you are already centering your life on the Lord and focusing your time and energy on Him. As we agreed, you and I, dear mom, are to love the Lord and His Word. We are to be God's kind of *women,* which will make us God's kind of *moms.* God's instructions to parents begin "and these words which I command you today shall be in *your* heart" (Deuteronomy 6:6). When this is true of our hearts, we can successfully teach the Word of God to our children.

> *He who teaches the Bible is never a scholar; he is always a student.*

Christian Education 101

Do you think you need to have a teaching degree, credentials, or experience in order to do what God asks of His moms in the Bible? Well, good news! You don't! All you need is a heart eager to answer God's call to you in Deuteronomy 6:7. God does not require anything of you but a heart that desires to follow after Him and obey His directive to teach your kids. He expects His moms to perform this important role:

> My son...do not forsake *the law of your mother* (Proverbs 1:8 and 6:20).

> The words of King Lemuel, the utterance which *his mother taught him* (Proverbs 31:1).

In the Bible, teaching almost appears to be the Number One duty of a Christian parent. The Bible instructs, if you love your children, teach them...and the earlier the better. So dear mom, teach your growing young ones...no matter what. Moms tell me all the time, "But my children don't want to have devotions. They don't want to sit and listen to me read the Bible or Bible storybooks to them." And my answer is always the same—"Give your children what they need, not what they want." You're the adult. You know what's best and what wisdom will be needed in the future. You are also in charge as "God's agent." You have a "mandate to act"[2] and to teach. This doesn't mean you shouldn't try to make your teaching enjoyable and interesting. Consult other moms and Sunday school teachers for ideas. And check out books and games to make your teaching time with your children fruitful and fun.

Your faithful teaching of your children gives them a base of information (God's truth) from which they can live their lives God's way. Your instruction equips them to function throughout life with wisdom and helps them avoid many mistakes and heartbreaks. Therefore the wise mom daily makes sure that her children hear the

Who is best taught? He who first learned from his mother.

THE TALMUD

instruction of the law of God, the Word of God.

From the Cradle to the Grave

How early does a mom after God's own heart begin teaching her little one? While researching Deuteronomy 6:7, I found this guideline based on Jewish customs: "The life of a Jew is religious from the cradle to the grave. In the room occupied by the mother and her newborn infant the rabbi puts a paper containing Psalm 121 in Hebrew."[3] This particular psalm is one of powerful assurance that God is our helper, keeper, protector, and preserver throughout all of life.

Imagine the heart, faith, and emotion of the mom who holds her baby and prays Psalm 121 over her newborn—"The LORD is your keeper...your shade at your right hand. ...The LORD shall preserve you from all evil; He shall preserve your soul...your going out and your coming in from this time forth, and even forevermore....He will not allow your foot to be moved; He who keeps you will not slumber...nor sleep" (verses 5-8,3-4).

Here's a moving instance of a mom with a heart for teaching God's Word to her child "from the cradle." I heard about it when I attended a fund-raising luncheon for a crisis pregnancy center. At that gathering, the woman in charge moved us as an audience when she told us about a pregnant unmarried teen who became a Christian through the ministry of this particular center.

The expectant—and forgiven and grateful-to-God mom-to-be began memorizing Bible verses for her own soul...and then started to think about the baby on its way. So she began saying and reciting her verses to her tummy and the little unseen person there.

As her birth date approached, this teen girl (who was growing into a woman after God's own heart) asked for and received permission from the hospital where she would give birth to carry her memory verses into the delivery room. Why did she ask such a thing? Because she wanted the first sound her baby heard to be the Word of God. She wanted to hold the seconds-old infant in her arms and read—teach—aloud God's Word from Minute One, Day One, Word One of that little one's life.

Now, that's a mom after God's own heart! A mom can never begin too early to *teach* God's Word *diligently to her children.*

"Whetting" a Child's Heart

Exactly what does it mean to teach God's commands diligently to your children? Some say this instruction from Deuteronomy 6:7 could read, *"Thou shalt 'whet' them diligently upon thy children."* Spiritually speaking, to "whet" means to frequently repeat God's words to your children, to try any and every way of instilling the Scriptures into their minds and making them pierce into their hearts.

Here's the way it goes. We know that to whet a knife, it is turned first on this side, then on that, and stroked again and again, slowly and systematically, across the sharpening stone. In this same way faithful parents are to carefully and persistently teach the Bible to their children. Their aim is to sharpen them spiritually, to put a godly edge on them.[4] The repeated efforts of faithful parents will stimulate their children's appetites for the "milk" and, eventually, the "solid food"—meat—of the Word of God (Hebrews 5:12-14 and 1 Peter 2:2).

Yes, but How?

God not only tells us to teach our children, but He is faithful to also tell us *how* and *what* to teach them.

Verbal instruction—First on God's list in Deuteronomy 6 is audible, verbal instruction—"you shall teach them diligently to your children" (verse 7). We'll cover informal verbal instruction in the next chapter when we address what it means to "talk" of God's Word. But for now, I want to focus on the formal and verbal teaching of the Bible to your child.

The curriculum moms are to teach is, first and foremost, the Bible. As the school among the Jews was called "the house of the book,"[5] so your home must be "the home of the Book." And it helps to have a time that's set aside and scheduled for reading the Bible, a time when some part of the Bible is read out loud. It doesn't matter for how long it's read. Even a few minutes a day will make a powerful impression on your family. You can read from

*Pray, "Great Teacher—
God, oh, make Thou me the teacher that I long to be!"*[6]

the books of Psalms or Proverbs, a Gospel (Matthew, Mark, Luke, John), or from any book in the Bible...or even share a portion of a chapter of the Bible. Just be sure you read.

And don't worry about what your children are or are not getting out of your Bible reading times. What they do get is the firsthand experience of seeing your love for the Bible and your wholehearted commitment to God and His Son. They'll realize God's Word is important to you...therefore it will become important to them. They also get to hear the scriptures. And, as the Bible teaches, "faith comes by hearing, and hearing by the word of God" (Romans 10:17). Your family members also receive a familiarity and respect for the Bible that will help them to love and live the Word of God as they age.

Visual instruction—God also points to the importance of visual teaching and reminders. Regarding His commandments, God instructed those in Moses' day to "bind them as a sign on your hand, and they shall be as frontlets between your eyes. You shall write them on the doorposts of your house and on your gates" (Deuteronomy 6:8-9). To obey these instructions, God's people actually wore literal one-inch square boxes on their hands and heads that contained portions of God's law. They also inscribed sentences from the Torah on the lintels and posts of their doors. These were meant to remind them of "the unseen Guest in the house Whose presence should control and hallow all that is said and done in it."[7]

Today we, as New Testament believers, don't need to literally follow these guidelines. That's because God's Word sinks deep into our hearts. It is "written not with ink but by the Spirit of the living God, not on tablets of stone but on tablets of flesh, that is, of the heart" made, not of stone, but of flesh (2 Corinthians 3:3). But still there is a place for visual reminders of God's Word. For instance...

> I've met teenagers who wear a "purity ring" on their wedding band finger to remind them to stay pure until they are married, to "abstain from sexual immorality," and to keep their bodies "in sanctification and honor, not in passion of lust, like [those] who do not know God" (1 Thessalonians 4:3-5).
>
> Other people I know (including adults, teens, and children) wear bracelets with the initials "WWJD" to remind them to always ask the question—in any and every situation—"What Would Jesus Do?"
>
> One mom of a household of teens tacked up a plaque on the doorframe to her kitchen that cited Joshua's declaration of devotion to God in Joshua 24:15: "As for me and my house, we will serve the LORD." She told me, "The members of my family probably pass through the kitchen doorway a hundred times every day. Seeing this verse gives us a

hundred good daily reminders of Whom it is we serve."

Adults and kids alike display plaques, posters, and framed art in their rooms at home, on their computers, and in their work places that feature Bible prayers and verses of Scripture. In our house, I hung a number of scriptures on our walls that I embroidered and framed.

I'm sure you can add to this list of visual instruction and reminders of our Great God, and please do! But what am I saying? Or rather, what is God saying to us as parents, as moms, in Deuteronomy 6:7? By now we know the answer. He is telling us to "teach" His Word and His commands "diligently" to our children—"to drill"[8] them into their hearts and minds.

Heart Response

As a mom, there is no one you love more on this earth than your children (and of course, their dad!). And teaching your children about God and His ways is not optional. God is assigning and authorizing you to teach His Word to your children steadily and purposefully, all day long, everyday at home...and everywhere else. You're a mom on a mission! Therefore, instructing those you love most in the things of the God you love supremely should be—or become—a passion and a pleasure.

And remember, if you begin to wonder how much to teach or waver in your teaching, your children can *never* get enough teaching from the Bible! So set a regular time to instruct your kids in God's Word and His principles. Even if you are getting a late start, start now. If your children are older and wonder, "What happened to Mom?" be bold. Tell them there's been a wonderful change in your heart, and you want to start a little Bible time because it will help them too.

Mom, the particular stage of your life or your kids' lives doesn't matter. Just read! Read God's Word together until it becomes familiar to your boys and girls, until the Bible becomes a cherished friend and a trusted guide. Read it to them until, hopefully, it is written—burned, etched, and recorded—deeply on the tablet of each of their hearts (Proverbs 3:3). A child after God's own heart is shaped and formed as the Word of God becomes embedded into his or her heart, mind, and character. As a poet expresses it,

> Whatever you write on the heart of a child
> No water can wash away.
> The sand may be shifted when billows are wild
> And the efforts of time may decay.
>
> Some stories may perish, some songs be forgot
> But this graven record—time changes it not.
> Whatever you write on the heart of a child...
> Will linger unchangeably there.[9]

From a Dad's Heart

What a wonderful privilege you have as a mom after God's own heart! You are blessed to not only bring your children into the world, but also to bring them up in the nurture and admonition of the Lord! So regardless of where your husband is on the "religion scale," you must do all you can to teach your children about God with the following cautions in mind.

If your husband is not a believer, make sure you are discreet about your teaching. Don't be an in-your-face Christian wife. Also don't purposefully use your children to manipulate your husband into some kind of faith. If the children are excited about what you are teaching them and they naturally share it with their father, let the Holy Spirit do His work through your children's enthusiasm. Otherwise, quietly, behind the scenes, instruct your children in the things of God. You have many opportunities when your husband is not at home or is busy at home. This instruction should include showing loving respect to their dad, whatever he does or doesn't believe about God.

If you do have a believing husband, thank God every day for this man! Your job of teaching becomes a little easier. Most men are busy providing for their families, so they don't always think about the teaching aspect of being a parent. I know Elizabeth was very diligent to assist me in doing my part in training up our girls. She would have the Bible and our daily devotional book at my place at the breakfast table each morning. The next devotional reading was well marked—just in case I had forgotten the place from the day before. She would always structure the early morning so there was time for family devotions before we all went off in a hundred different directions.

Then in the evenings when I was home, Elizabeth would schedule my time with the girls as part of the evening ritual. No pressure. Just simple nonverbal reminders of my responsibility to be part of the "team" of teachers to train up our girls.

Why not sit down with your husband and agree on the part each of you is to play in the exciting role of teaching your children about God? The reward is great! I'm so blessed as I see my daughters now doing many of the same things with their husbands that my wife (and their mom) did with me! And the ultimate reward? My grandchildren are hearing the Word of God not only from their moms but also from their dads.

*L*ittle *C*hoices That Reap Big Blessings

1. Read God's Word regularly yourself.

Oh, dear mom! Your personal love of and familiarity with the Scriptures will be a driving force in your desire to share it with your children and in your faithful follow-through on God's calling to do so. When God's Word fills your heart, you won't be able to wait to pass on the most important thing in the world to your little and big ones! As you fall more in love with God's Word, you'll want your children to do the same. So be sure the first little choice on your to-do list each day is your own heart-filling, soul-refreshing, strength-producing time with your Bible. Choose to do it for yourself...and choose to do it for your family.

2. Read from the Bible first.

As a busy mom of a family that runs on a variety of schedules, there's only so much time that can be found for reading together. So when that precious (and scheduled!) time comes around, be sure you treat the Bible as the most important book in the world. After all, it is *The Book!* Even if you read Christian books and literature to your brood, make sure the Bible is treated as the most important book they will ever hear or read. And if you only have time to read from one book, you know what to do—make sure you choose the Bible! Other books, as good and solid and helpful as they may be, are, quite simply, not the Word of God. They are about the Word of God or drawn from the Word of God. Nothing can take the place of the God-breathed, God-inspired, written-by-God-Himself Scriptures (2 Timothy 3:16). They and they alone are quick and powerful and "sharper than any two-edged sword" (Hebrews 4:12). And they and they alone are "profitable for doctrine, for reproof, for correction, for instruction in righteousness, that the man of God may be complete, thoroughly equipped for every good work" (2 Timothy 3:16).

And here's something else—Be sure each of your children has a Bible, no matter what their ages. They can bring it to the table, take it to church, carry it around all day, sleep with it...whether they can read it or not! (What a great baby shower gift!)

And something else—Read the Bible to your kids, no matter what their ages. Remember, even an infant responds to its mother's voice. If you begin early, your child will never know what it's like to not hear the Bible being read out loud.

3. Read Christian books to your family.

Borrow good Christian books that reinforce and illustrate the truths from the Bible. Check them out from your church library or borrow them from friends. Get your hands on anything that is centered on the Bible and appropriate for your children's ages. Every child—even teens—loves to hear about God's "superheroes" of the Bible. And children are mesmerized by rhymed versions of the Bible and its exciting truths. Read these books over and over with your children until they are familiar favorites and their messages become a point of reference for their actions, choices, and character. Make it a point to read them at meals, at snack times, after school, at bedtime. Again, your little—and big ones—can never get enough teaching from and about the Bible. In time, you may even want to build your own library of cherished favorites.

4. Read to everyone.

I urge you, don't leave anyone out! Pay no attention to your children's ages. And if they have friends over, include them too. Just pile the whole kit and caboodle of kids into the room, on the bed, the floor, the couch, or around the table, and read away! One of my favorite pictures of my family is my son-in-law reading to five of our grandchildren on a little toddler bed. All the kids, representing a rainbow of ages, are enveloped into Paul's arms and leaning on one another...and hanging on every word out of his mouth. I call this picture "Paul's Bible Club." He does this every bedtime with his children and is always faithful and happy to include all of the family members whenever we get together.

5. Read from Proverbs.

God states the purpose of the book of Proverbs right up front in chapter one, verse four: "To give...the young man knowledge and discretion." From that point on, Solomon (the writer) addresses "my son" at least 23 times. You see, Solomon wrote the book of Proverbs to teach his child—his young son—wisdom, to instruct him in the disciplines he would need throughout life. So give your children the gift of the proverbs. Give them godly wisdom. How? Read out loud from the proverbs at every opportunity.

3

Talk to Your Children About God

*And these words
which I command you today
shall be in your heart.
You shall...talk of them
when you sit in your house,
when you walk by the way,
when you lie down, and
when you rise up.*

DEUTERONOMY 6:6-7

What does your average day look like? It's very, *very* busy, right? But despite a hectic pace, it also probably falls into some sort of schedule or routine. Most moms' days begin with the sound of an alarm clock...or a crying baby. Then things begin to rock and roll! There are others to wake up, breakfast to fix, people to get settled or out the door and off to work or school, household tasks to take care of, not to mention errands, evening meal preparations, carpooling, extracurricular activities for everyone, home-schooling...and perhaps even your own job.

Well, in the midst of all of the above—and more!—God helps you do two things at the same time. All of the busyness of your personal and family life must be managed and taken care of, but so must teaching your children about our almighty and awesome God. How can a swamped momma fit this assignment into an already brimming and impossible schedule? Well, thank the Lord that He comes to the rescue and prescribes His all-wise solution! He says:

> And these words which I command you today shall be in your heart. You shall...*talk* of them when you sit in your house, when you walk by the way, when you lie down, and when you rise up (Deuteronomy 6:6-7).

God doesn't ask or require that you have any special giftedness, training, degrees, or abilities to further instruct your children in the things of God. No, regardless of your background, upbringing, or education, you can effectively point your little (and big!) ones' hearts toward God. All you have to do is *talk* about Him all day long. Just talk about God in the ebb and flow of the day-in, day-out rhythm of normal (albeit chaotic!) home life. (Now we're talking, because "talking" is something we women excel at. And it's something God is asking us to do for Him and for our children's sakes!)

Speak Up!

God tells us moms clearly and simply what He wants us to do. He says "you shall...*talk* of them." And what is the *them?* "These words which I command you" (verse 6). And who is it you are to talk to? Primarily, your children...and anyone and everyone else who will listen. With these instructions God is asking you and His corps of godly moms to constantly focus all of everyday life on Him and His teachings. And how is this done? It's easy! By *talking* about the things of God with your children *while* you go through the bedlam of each crazy day.

It takes dedicated parents to produce consecrated children.

Again, looking to the Jewish model, we learn that the Hebrews made religion a built-in part of life. And the reason for their success was that religious education was life-oriented, not just information-oriented. They used the context of daily life as opportunities to teach about God and to talk of Him. They purposefully pointed all of life back to God, ingraining God's teachings into their children's hearts.

Do you want your children to love God? Then simply talk about Him. Why talk about God? Because we talk about what's important to us. And when we don't talk about God, we send a loud message to our children that God really isn't that important. So make God a part of your everyday life and chit-chat. Talk about Him and His ways. Talk about His Word and His Son. Talk about the wonder of His creation. This act of talking will make God a part of your children's everyday experiences and conversations.

So take note: God is asking you to commit yourself to teach your children diligently to see Him in all aspects of life, not just those that are church related. Your teaching is to go on no matter where you are physically with your children.

And what will happen? You never know! But here are a few assurances. When you speak of God,

♡ You honor and glorify Him.

♡ You obey His teaching to talk of Him to your children.

♡ You are spiritually uplifted as you voice your heart for God and your knowledge of Him.

♡ Your chances for positively affecting and infecting your family by your communication go sky high!

As I said, you never know what wonderful things will happen as you faithfully obey God, so speak up! It's been reported that the renowned and eloquent preacher Dr. G. Campbell Morgan had four sons who all became ministers. At a family reunion, a friend asked one of the sons, "Which Morgan is the greatest preacher?" While the son directly looked at his famous father, he replied, "Mother." Obviously this man-of-God had a mom-of-God who followed after God's own heart and Deuteronomy 6:6-7...and spoke up.

Dear mom, speak up!

Speak Up Day and Night

God goes on and tells you *when* to speak up and talk to your children. It's to be done "when you sit in your house, when you walk by the way, when you lie down, and when you rise up" (Deuteronomy 6:7).

In other words, as you and your little family sit in your house, while you do your work, when you are relaxing, when you are eating...talk about the Lord. Or when you are resting, or when you tuck in the kids as they lie down at night to sleep, or when someone has a bad dream in the night or is sick...talk about the Lord. And when you first awake to the gift of yet another glorious day God has given...talk about the Lord. Even when you visit or talk with others, when you walk by the way and go through your day, when you run your errands, and when you do your housework...talk about the Lord. Take every occasion as an opportunity to talk with your children about divine things, about the plain and simple truths and laws of God. For instance...

Did you see a rainbow today? Are the seasons changing? Did it snow? Was the sky clear at night, giving you a glimpse of the moon and the stars? Remark with wonder, "Only God can make a rainbow! It's a sign of His goodness!...For everything there is a season!...God's heavens declare the glory of God!"

Are you doling out, checking up on, or praising your kids' work chores? Spout out the teachings of Proverbs and God's work ethic—"There is profit in all labor!...The hand of the diligent will rule!"[1]

Are you fixing a meal together or setting the table with the children? Remind them that God takes care of His own, that He promises to supply all their needs...

forever. Share with them that they will never hunger or thirst and that God promises He will even prepare a table for them in the presence of enemies!

Is everyone under your roof getting along with each other? Whether they are—or aren't—speak constantly of God's instructions to be kind to others, to do to others (including their brothers and sisters!) whatever they would want done to them.

The Bible says the godly (that's you, mom!) are to meditate on the scriptures at all times. And "blessed" is the one (you again!) whose "delight is in the law of the LORD, and in His law he meditates day and night" (Psalm 1:2). And the Bible says you, precious mom after God's own heart, are to talk of Him day and night to your children.

That's the picture in Deuteronomy 6. And that's what God wants to be true of you and your family. What a great way to spend every day of your life—reveling in the God you love and talking about Him all day long with those you love most!

It's Never Too Early...

I was struck to the core as a young mom (...who got a late start on Christian parenting!) when I read a devotional that began with a United Press newspaper release that heralded "the time to start a child on a musical career isn't too far beyond the bootie and bottle age." I read on to discover that a world-famous violin teacher in Japan believed that the earlier a child is exposed to music, the better a musician he will be. Dr. Shinichi Suzuki stated that "just as a child imitates gestures, he can also imitate music." He then prescribed, "For this reason it is extremely important that a child hear *nothing but good music from a very early age*." Therefore, although Dr. Suzuki likes to start his students in classes between the ages of two and four, he begins exposing them to music even earlier.[2]

And then I thought about my two little ones...who were one-and-a-half and two-and-a-half before I even became a Christian mom. Oh, how I wanted to begin to influence them for Christ right away. And I didn't have a second to lose! I prayed to God that, being a late-bloomer in the Christian Education Department at home, it wouldn't be too late!

I mean, here was a man, a teacher of *music*, saying that "it is extremely important that a child hear *nothing but* good music from a very early age" so that he will mimic only the best! How much more important—no, critical!—it is that our children who come to us from the mind and heart and hand of God hear *nothing but good* in our Christian homes. The apostle Paul wrote concerning Timothy, "that from *childhood* you have known the Holy Scriptures" (2 Timothy 3:15). I pray the same will be true of you and your beloved family. May your children hear and learn about God from childhood!

All of this to say, dear mom, start them early. It's never too early to begin sharing God's words and teachings with your little ones. Go ahead...talk your head off!

...And It's Never Too Late

And, at the same time, it's never too late. Did you know that...

Ninety-one percent of all 13-year-olds, whether they are exposed to Christian truth or not, pray to God during a typical week?

Most adolescents are involved in religious activity of some sort?

Nine out of 10 young people accept the existence of God, and 91 percent accept the fact that every person has an eternal soul?

More than 4 out of 5 youths want to have a close relationship with God as a cornerstone in their lives?

Two-thirds of American teens are at least somewhat persuaded that the Bible is totally accurate in its teachings.[3]

This survey data reveals that teens—and even college-age young adults—do want to know what to believe and also want to believe what their parents believe.

Dear mom, others—including the enemy!—will be happy to tell you it's too late to begin teaching your older kids about God. But never ever forget that with God nothing is impossible. He will be faithful to honor and bless your faithful obedience to follow His Word.

So determine right this second to begin talking about the things of God "when you sit in your house, when you walk by the way, when you lie down, and when you rise up." Then, hopefully, your little—and big—ones will mimic what they are hearing and learning from your heart and lips about your Lord.

How Important Is God to You?

But there is a core issue. As a mom and grandmom, I ask myself these questions regularly, and now I share them with you: How important is God and His Son to you? And how important is nurturing godly character in your life? Are you emulating God's standards to your family?

An author shared this frightening information: "One survey I read asked parents...which quality they most desired in their children. *Intelligence* topped the list, followed closely by *personality*, then *creativity*, and *imagination*." He then wondered, "What ever happened to trust, love, faith, honesty...? Aren't those the real building blocks for maturity?"[4]

I know this is soul-searching. But go ahead and ask—and answer—the tough questions. Think about what you talk about with your kids. What do you point them toward? (Do you ask "What will others think?" or "What does God desire?") What activities do you reward the most? (Excelling at school or kindness to brothers and sisters?) What achievements thrill you most? (A's or another memorized verse?) What groups do you encourage them to follow? (Being on the pep squad or being faithful to attend their Christian youth group?) What endeavors do you push them to pursue? (Soccer/gymnastics or the Bible programs or clubs at church?) What accomplishments make you happiest? (A good report card or a consistent personal quiet time?)

Don't get me wrong. There is nothing wrong with excelling at school, or being a part of school programs and activities, or participating in sports and physical

*Imitate me,
just as I also
imitate Christ.*

1 CORINTHIANS 11:1

activity. But do lay your answers next to the teaching of Deuteronomy 6:6-7. Then pray and make any changes that are needed...right away. Remember, it's not too late for you to change the direction of your emphasis at home. (I'll be sharing my own turnaround story in a little bit.) It's not too late to commit yourself to the priority of teaching God's Word, of talking about Him, of pointing all of life toward Him. Doing so will affect your children's hearts and lives!

Heart Response

Of course we should talk *to* God about our children. That's a given. But we should—and must—also talk to our children *about* God. That's the instruction of Deuteronomy 6:6-7. God expects—and assigns—us to talk to our sons and daughters about God at all times. He asks us as moms to take every opportunity to talk about Him—and also make the instances in life an opportunity to talk about Him and His Son.

Talk about "home" schooling! Many moms today are choosing to school their children at home. In fact, one of my daughters is taking this route with her oldest. But whether you homeschool or not, you are called to "homeschool" your children in the things of the Lord. Home is the best school for teaching the biblical precepts the Bible teaches and those your family stands for. And again, you are to teach and to talk of God and His Word to your kids all day long...every day...as often as you can...and for as long as you can.

And there's an urgency! In the context of Deuteronomy 6, God is expressing the absolute importance of His Word to His people through Moses. It was so important that He instructed His people to do everything possible to know, keep, and remember His commands. He wanted them incorporated into everyday life. And He wanted all parents to pass them on to the next generation...who were to pass them on to the next...and the next...and the next.

So, you see, now, as well as then, the spiritual education of children was the responsibility of the parents. Sure, others help. Godly pastors and Sunday-school teachers and youth lead-

> *Spiritual and moral principles are best conveyed in the laboratory of life.*[5]

ers and mentors contribute mightily. And Christian schools partner with you in teaching God's Word and ways to your children. But *you*, dear mom, as a parent are the one (along with your husband if he participates in your passion for Christ) who is called to wholeheartedly embrace God's instruction to teach and talk to your children about Him...and to faithfully live it out in the everyday setting of life at home and in the world.

So, once again, we've come full circle, right back to *your* love for God, Mom, haven't we? "*You* shall love the LORD your God with all *your* heart, with all *your* soul, and with all *your* strength. And these words which I command you today shall be in *your* heart" (Deuteronomy 6:5-6). That's Step One.

And here is Step Two: "*You* shall teach them diligently to your children...and *[you]* shall talk of them when you sit in your house, when you walk by the way, when you lie down, and when you rise up." And when you do, my precious fellow-mom, you show forth *your* love for God. For as His Son said, "If you love Me, keep My commandments" (John 14:15).

From a Dad's Heart

I can still remember the day Elizabeth learned about the importance of singing hymns and praise songs and talking openly about God with our little girls. She came home from her mom's Bible study and immediately shared it with me. As we began to follow this wise advice and establish this practice, I was amazed to discover that our kids' little minds were sponges. They soaked up everything they came into contact with.

I was also shocked after we became a Christian family to learn that, at one-and-a-half and two-and-a-half, our girls had already missed out on some vital years of Christian training! (As Elizabeth said, it's never too early to begin talking about God.)

But I'm also grateful that by God's grace it's never too late. Even though Elizabeth and I felt we were behind in talking about God, we started where we and the children were. And this is my advice to you too. Don't become immobilized by past mistakes, failures, or inactivity. Thank God for what you are learning now...today. Then with newfound vitality and renewed vigor and excitement for the Lord, start "talking up God." Your enthusiasm can't help but rub off on your family!

And here's another suggestion: If your husband is interested, and the timing is good (that's very important when talking to us guys!), share this chapter with him. A father can contribute much emotionally and physically to the children and to the home. But everything he does around the home *spiritually* seems to get double mileage. When Dad comes home, the children listen. And because he's Dad, they *really* watch what he does and says. So, in your sweet way, try to alert him to the importance of talking about God, talking about Jesus, talking about being a Christian. Ask him to speak up. Believe me, it will make a lasting impression on the kids!

Sometimes it's hard for a guy to think of something spiritual to say. (That was me!) So one of the ways I became involved with the everyday Christian "talk" around our house was to help the girls memorize their verses for their church programs. I did this for more than a decade. Every day the girls and I would attempt to say "our" memory verses to each other. That would get us talking and sharing about what the verses meant and how each one could apply the verses in her personal life and at home and at school.

And here's another thing I did. I said earlier that I began to lead devotions each morning. And many times the daily devotional would spark a lively conversation at the breakfast table too. And there were also times when we would continue the discussion at dinner.

Even if your husband is one of those "stay silent type" guys, ask him to assist you spiritually when he is home. Ask him to simply talk about God to the children. Just maybe after he talks about God around the house, his faith will be strengthened and he'll want to go to work and talk about God there too!

Little Choices That Reap Big Blessings

1. Ask God to help you be more aware of Him.

In Deuteronomy, God begins with your heart, mom. He then moves to your calling to pass your heart for God along to your boys and girls. Ask Him for His help in making you more aware of Him—of His goodness, of His creation, of His love for you. If you want your children to follow God, make God a part of *your* everyday experiences.

2. Purpose to talk about the Lord.

Create an environment and a schedule or routine for teaching your children about God and the principles of Scripture. But go the next step and purpose to intentionally talk about God. One thing that has helped me as a mom (and as a Christian) has been trying to begin my sentences with the word "God" or with "the Lord." If you do this, you'll most definitely be talking of the Lord and relating all of life to Him.

3. Examine your daily routine for opportunities.

How do your waking-up hours go each morning? And how can you introduce and interject God into that portion of the day? And how do things generally flow when others are leaving the house in the morning for school or work? What could you do to leave them with some reminder of God? In our routine, we had a prayer circle at the front door every day when the first member of our family left for the day...followed by a group hug.

Are any little ones at home during the day? How can God be the center of their at-home time? You could have verses for them to memorize and illustrate with crayons or markers. Another option is to have a CD of children's hymns that can play in the background all day. Keep a plethora of Christian children's books lying all over the place (even if they come from the church library). Do you play videos or DVDs in your home? If so, do you have a storehouse of Christian videos to further fill their minds with teaching about God?

Are your children going off to public school? Oh, then you *must* send them off with some reminder of God. Send them into the world with a 3″ x 5″ card or a sticker or a bookmark or a verse in their lunch. And don't forget to pause and pray with them in the car as you drop them off. Then, when you pick them up after school or they come through the front door ask, "How did God bless your day?"

4. Center on God at mealtime.

Examine your mealtimes. Are you praying and saying "grace" and asking your children to partici- pate in the praying? A word of caution: Do be sensitive to your husband's desires. If he is not a Christian, don't push this issue. Just be sure you pray with your children of all ages at mealtime and snack time when your husband is not pres- ent.

5. End the day with God.

And how about the evenings? Again, be aware of your husband's desires for the nightly routine when he's there. But you can still have a quiet little individual talk with each of your loved ones, even your teens, when they go to bed. Remind them of a memory verse or truth about God. I especially loved ending each little bedtime talk with "Jesus loves you, and so do I." And today, I'm doing the same things with our next little gen- eration!

4

$\mathcal{T}$ell Your Children About Jesus

We are ambassadors for Christ,
as though God were pleading through us.

2 CORINTHIANS 5:20

'm looking at the cover of a book that's lying here on my desk as I write. It pictures a large archery target with an arrow imbedded in the target's bull's eye. The book addresses a different subject than we're focusing on in our book. But the graphics of the target, arrow, and bull's eye hit the mark when it comes to depicting the message of this chapter. It's right on! There are many "things" we moms must do to love our children. In fact, we're addressing ten of them in this book. But *the* most important one—"the bull's eye"—is that we must tell them about Jesus!

Aim for Your Child's Heart

First, there's the target. I know you live a multilayered life. I also know it's filled with the challenge of multi-tasking during every waking minute of every day! Your list of responsibilities is long. And so is the list of people you must care for. Truly, the number of hats you regularly wear is staggering!

But somewhere in the midst of all you do, want to do, and need to do, there should be this aim: to educate and introduce each of your children to Jesus Christ. You can't "save" them. Only God can do that. That's His job. But your job is to instruct young hearts in the truth about Jesus and His importance in their lives. You need to do everything imaginable to make them aware of God's Son and His message of salvation.

I'll go a step further and say, *You must see telling your kids about Jesus as your Number One priority and purpose in life as a mom*. Of course you're going to love them, feed them, and pray for them. But as a Christian mother who's been saved by Christ's sacrifice and God's grace, you are to be a full-fledged "ambassador for Christ" (2 Corinthians 5:20). You are a representative of Christ to your children, a spokesperson for God. And what is the message you are to bring to them? It's the same message Paul was sent to deliver in 2 Corinthians 5—"We implore you on Christ's behalf, be reconciled to God" (verse 20).

Here's a thought-provoking question: What do you consider to be the target of all that you do for your kids? What is the purpose and aim of your parenting? Take a look at your life and your priorities. What are you intent on teaching your children? How to tie their shoelaces?

Techniques in brushing and flossing? Good manners? How to catch, kick, or hit a ball? How to make an A? How to play an instrument? Respect for others and for property? The list could go on and on. But as good and as necessary as these issues and activities are in your kids' lives, what you must be asking your heart is, Am I making sure I tell them about Jesus? Until you and I wake up every single morning and know without doubt that "Today, if I don't get anything else done, I must teach my children about my Lord Jesus," we are aiming at the wrong target. So take aim!

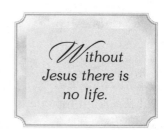

Without Jesus there is no life.

Directing the Truths About Jesus

Next come the arrows. What are the piercing arrows we want to sink into little hearts?

Obviously, they are the Scriptures. The truth. The Word of God. The Bible. And especially the Bible's account and stories about Jesus' life. Teach your children about Jesus—His miracles, His teachings, His birth, death, and resurrection, His interactions with His Father and His disciples, His goodness, His perfect, sinless life.

And what is the best way to accomplish this goal? It's simple! Read out loud to your children daily from the four Gospels—Matthew, Mark, Luke, and John. Have your kids share in the reading if they can. Also have them write out and memorize key verses such as, "Jesus said to him, 'I am the way, the truth, and the life. No one comes to the Father except through Me'" (John 14:6).

Even if your three-year-old can only scrawl out a few letters of the alphabet, have those letters be J-E-S-U-S. (And, of course, Step 2 could be "Jesus loves me.")

Also have your family work puzzles and anagrams. Encourage them to write letters and prayers to Jesus about what they are learning. Start a Jesus scrapbook. Set up a time for them to draw or color pictures of the stories you are reading to them about Jesus. Create a full-on craft time aimed at illustrating the day's story and truth.

For instance, this Christmas when our family got together, our focus was on the Christmas story in the Bible. To reinforce our emphasis I had purchased five sticker sheets (one for each little person) with stickers of the figures in the nativity scene. So one day our "craft for the day" was to use the stickers to recreate the Christmas story on a piece of construction paper.

You can well imagine the hodgepodge of places where Baby Jesus, the donkeys, camels, shepherds, and wise men ended up! And God's star did not always "appear" in the upper half of the paper. But this fun time served to reinforce the Bible's account of God sending His Son to live—and die—for us. What a joy to see five little minds and ten little hands (and, I pray, five little hearts!) handling each person and animal that had a part in Jesus' advent! And it only cost pennies.

Now, what will you do today or this week to direct the truths about Jesus toward little and big hearts?

Hitting the Bull's Eye

And what is the bull's eye? For me as a mom, I wanted my children to know God, to love my Jesus, and to enjoy the eternal life spoken of in 1 John 5:12:

> He who has the Son has life; he who does
> not have the Son of God does not have life.

So I prayed (and prayed and prayed!) for my girls to have a relationship with God through Christ. And I know you want the same for your flesh and blood. Therefore, to hit the bull's eye, take care to share vocally and repeatedly the facts about "the gospel."

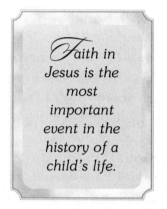

Faith in Jesus is the most important event in the history of a child's life.

What is the gospel? Here's a short answer. Paul, who received the gospel message from Christ Himself, was faithful to pass it on to others in 1 Corinthians 15:3-4. He put it this way, "For I delivered to you first of all that which I also received: that Christ died for our sins according to the Scriptures, and that He was buried, and that He rose again the third day according to the Scriptures."

As you can imagine, whole volumes have been written on these two verses. But for our sakes, think of the gospel truths presented in these three statements:

> *Christ died for our sins*—The sinless Jesus Christ bore the punishment of sin so that those who believe have their sins removed.
>
> *He was buried*—Jesus Christ died on a real cross and was buried in a real tomb.

He rose again the third day—God the Father raised Jesus Christ up from the dead, permanently and forever.

What does this mean to us and to our children? First of all, the Bible says that "all have sinned" (Romans 3:23). Clearly, then, we and our children are in need of forgiveness for sin. We need a Savior! We need Jesus! The Bible also says "godly sorrow" over sin "produces repentance [a desire to turn from sin and restore one's relationship with God] leading to salvation" (2 Corinthians 7:10).

All of that said, mom, speak from your heart and from God's Word to your children. Make it a point every day. See it as a sacred, nonoptional, daily duty. Praise your children's good deeds, but be faithful to point out any behavior that goes against God's standards. And at the same time, point them to Jesus as the One who can forgive their sins and help them do the right things. Talk to them about Jesus' death for their sins. And share the good news that He is alive—that they can have life in Him and live forever in His presence. Let them know the promise of John 1:12: "But as many as received Him, to them He gave the right to become children of God, to those who believe in His name."

Build a bridge of truth to your child's heart and pray for Jesus to walk over it.

Here's what Jim and I did with our little ones. For several years our family sang in unison and with gusto the hymn that expresses, "When we all get to heaven what a day of rejoicing that will be!"...until one day Jim said, "Wait a minute! How do we all get to heaven?"

That's when we began teaching and telling our girls more about Jesus. We started to share the truths I've mentioned, as well as what I call "either or" truths:

> Enter by the narrow gate; for wide is the gate and broad is the way that leads to destruction, and there are many who go in by it (Matthew 7:13).

> He who has the Son has life; he who does not have the Son of God does not have life (1 John 5:12).

> Unless one is born again, he cannot see the kingdom of God (John 3:3).

Again, only God can save your child's soul. And only God can work in your child's heart. But His Spirit works through His arrows—His Word and His truth. Be ever faithful to do your part. You must preach Christ! As the apostle Paul remarked, "How then shall they call on Him in whom they have not believed? And how shall they believe in Him of whom they have not heard? And how shall they hear without a preacher?" (Romans 10:14).

Well, that's you, mom. You are to be one of God's "preachers of the gospel." And your little flock is right there at home! So make telling your children about Jesus the priority purpose and aim of your parenting. Be faithful to open your mouth. Be faithful to prepare. Be faithful to teach. And be faithful to preach! Be faithful to hang in there and persist...while being faithful to live out genuine faith. And, of course, be faithful to pray!

But What If...?

Are you wondering, "But what if my child has already prayed to receive Jesus as Savior?" First, that is great news! But now "the target" becomes spiritual growth. And spiritual growth is progressive and ongoing. Each new day and trial will bring you more opportunities to teach your child about Jesus—how He grew, how He knew the Scriptures, how He walked through life and trouble, how He treated others, how He prayed, how He loved and obeyed—and trusted—the Father, how He lived fully for God, how He fulfilled God's purpose for Him.

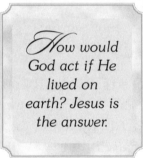

How would God act if He lived on earth? Jesus is the answer.

The Bible says, "But grow in the grace and knowledge of our Lord and Savior Jesus Christ" (2 Peter 3:18). Let your family members respond to each truth along the way. Also have them articulate their understanding of the gospel and their beliefs to you. This way you can keep your finger on the spiritual pulse of each child. You'll also gain insights into the level of their understanding, which will lead and guide you in further conversations about God.

When Should You Start?

Moms ask me regularly if such-and-such age is too soon to begin telling little ones about Jesus. And my answer (as you know by now!) is always the same—it's never too early to start. In fact, may your children never remember a day when you didn't talk to them about Jesus, your Best Friend and Savior!

Consider, too, these survey results: "People are much more likely to accept Christ as their Savior when they are young. Absorption of biblical information and principles typically peaks during the preteen years....Habits related to the practice of one's faith develop when one is young and change surprisingly little over time."[1]

Your goal, then, as a Christian mom is to teach and teach and teach your children about Jesus. To share and share and share with them about Him! To talk and talk and talk about the Savior. English preacher and evangelist C.H. Spurgeon rhymed it this way:

> Ere a child has reached to seven
> Teach him all the way to heaven;
> Better still the work will thrive
> If he learns before he's five.

Never Give Up!

Is your child older than five? Or seven? Or the preteens? Don't despair! Instead check your heart (and emotions!) and do the following:

> *Remember*—salvation is God's job, His work in your older child's heart.
>
> *Pray*—fervently for your older son or daughter and faithfully to "God our Savior, who desires all men to be saved and to come to the knowledge of the truth" (1 Timothy

2:3-4). And pray for him or her until you die. Aim the arrows of your prayers for any wayward or lagging children heavenward until your last dying breath. It's never too late to pray! And it's never too late for the miracle of salvation!

Talk—to your teens and young adults about Christ. Point the issues in their lives back to Jesus—His teachings, His life, His wisdom, and His ability to help...and to save. Even if they say, "Oh, mom, there you go again!" go right ahead and talk about Jesus. They act like they couldn't care less but, believe me, it's going in! And they are having to process it. I ask you, if they are not going to hear it from *you*, the one who lives with them and loves them most, then *who?* You, dear faithful mom, are the one closest to any of your children who desperately need to hear and know about Jesus.

> *The gospel breaks hard hearts.*

I've shared before in one of my books about Augustine, cited to be "one of the greatest of the Church Fathers."[2] For 33 years Augustine scorned the Christian teaching and prayers of his mother, Monica. And yet Monica never gave up. She preached. She prayed. She pursued...until one day, at age 33, Augustine cried out in agony to God, "How long? Remember not the sins of my youth!" When he told his mom he had at last embraced the Savior, Monica said, "Now I can die in peace." Her son's salvation was the only thing on earth she had desired. Monica died five days later, and her son went on from having been a prodigal to becoming a pillar in the church.

Never give up!

As a mom after God's own heart who's been blessed by Him to have children, you are also appointed by Him to share the knowledge of His Son with each child under your roof. If you never get beyond this one priority—this one target!—in your lifetime, you will live a full and meaningful life. Even if all your other dreams pass you by, doing this one thing will be enough...because *this* is what God asks of you as one of His moms.

And, whatever you do, don't get caught up in worrying about your children's responses to the truth about Jesus. I know you care passionately and pray fervently about their eternal souls, and that's natural...and a good thing! But again, salvation is God's job. But here's what you can do: Open your heart to God and own His assignment to you to tell your children about Him—about His love—and about His precious Son. Accept this as a calling from God. Embrace it and go forward full-speed ahead. And do so with confidence and zeal!

Dear mom, this is *the big why* when it comes to all we do for our children. Why do we teach them God's Word, talk to them about God, take them to church, train them in God's ways, teach them to pray, and talk to God about them? We do it because it's our God-given responsibility, our role, our duty, and our mandate from God. Our heart's desire—indeed, the goal of our life—is that our children hear the truths about Christ. And then, Lord willing and by His grace, we pray that those truths will strike deeply into their hearts, that they may come to know Christ personally and enjoy the promise of eternal life!

So roll up your sleeves and move out heartily on your mission! Take great care—and exact aim—and target the heart of each of your loved ones. Pummel the hearts of those under your roof again and again with truth after truth about Jesus. And do it for years! Pray with each truth that the knowledge of sin, salvation, and the need for a Savior will sink deeply into soft young hearts...until, by God's grace, they respond positively.

From a Dad's Heart

As a former pastor I conducted many sessions of marriage counseling. As a general rule, the couples I talked with fell into two groups.

The first category was what the Bible calls being "unequally yoked" (2 Corinthians 6:14), where one partner is not a Christian. If your husband is not a Christian, he won't be all that interested in hearing about Jesus. But he is probably very interested in knowing that the children are under control. He likes knowing that the home is clean. And he *loves* knowing what's for dinner! For this dear guy, make sure you are living out before him the reality of the Jesus you want him and your children to know. Communication takes on many forms. Often we teach the loudest by what we do rather than what we say. Your actions will teach your husband about Jesus too! As the Bible says, "without a word" husbands "may be won by the conduct of their wives" (1 Peter 3:1).

The second category is a couple made up of two Christians. Now, and always, if you have a believing husband, thank God every day for this man and pray daily for growth and wisdom for him. Then beyond that, sit down with him in a quiet place and share what you are learning about being a mom after God's own heart. Let him know of your commitment to tell your children about Jesus. Share your dreams that they come to a genuine faith in Christ. Enlist his support in helping you talk about Christ.

Also be sure you thank him for all that he has already done to lift up the name of Jesus in the home. Thank him for the support and encouragement he has already given you in this critical task.

And if he is lagging behind in his understanding and efforts, tell him how important this assignment from the Lord is to you and how it should be to the both of you. Ask him for suggestions as to how the two of you can get the message of Jesus across to the hearts and minds of your children. Neither of you has all the answers and wisdom. However God has given you both the resources of godly men and women to help. Let your husband know you are willing to meet with a more seasoned woman for advice and wisdom. Then ask him if he would consider seeking out a more mature man in the church who has been down this road in the past.

I know this is where Elizabeth and I found ourselves in our early days of Christian parenting. We didn't have a clue about how to be godly parents. And we sure didn't know how to begin teaching our girls about Jesus. Elizabeth and I determined to go to as many parents as we could to ask for advice. And we did that until they got married.

Don't limp along in your parenting. Don't go it alone. Enlist your husband's help and the help of others in your church.

Little Choices That Reap Big Blessings

1. Concentrate on the gospel.

Now that you've thought about the power of the gospel message to salvation, do what my Jim did. Ask your kids, "But wait a minute! How do we all get to heaven?" Then choose to aim the arrows of the gospel more precisely, to pull the bow with more force, and to fire away more often. Consider this:

> The Gospel is God-given.
> The Gospel is what God does for man.
> The Gospel is good news.
> The Gospel ends in inner transformation.
> The Gospel is...a force—the power of God unto salvation.[3]

2. Share the lives of God's saints.

As you read Christian biographies with your kids, you'll find positive answer after positive answer about the difference knowledge of Jesus makes in a child's life and heart. For instance, think about the life of G. Campbell Morgan. He was a little boy who grew up to become a famous British minister and later the pastor of the Tabernacle Presbyterian Church in Philadelphia. Of him it is written that he was "a great organizer, a powerful preacher, a prince among evangelists, a teacher and leader amongst ministers and student of Holy Scriptures."[4]

But hear Mr. Morgan's own words: "My dedication to the preaching of the Word was maternal.... When but eight years old I preached to my little sister and to her dolls arrayed in orderly form before me. My sermons were Bible stories which I had first heard from my mother."[5]

Read on, mom! Tell your children the stories about Jesus from the Bible!

3. Sing about Jesus.

I was appalled one Sunday at church when I went to check on one of my small grandchildren. And there he was, sitting on the lap of a young girl who was assisting in the class. She was holding my grandson's hands and clapping them together singing "MIC-KEY M-O-U-S-E" to him. I smiled and quietly (I hope!) asked, "Do you know "Jesus Loves Me"? When she answered "Sure," I said, "That's one of his favorites. Why don't you sing that with him? He loves that one."

Oh, how my heart hurt! Here we were, as a Christian family, bringing everyone to church so they could learn more about Jesus. But I got a message too: When at home sing about Jesus! I wondered how many times I missed an opportunity to sing or tell that same toddler more about Jesus!

4. Budget for books.

It's staggering how much a family can pay for cable TV service, videos, and CDs. So don't hesitate to have a budget for Jesus books. Schedule regular visits to your Christian bookstore and keep a list of the titles you spot on your outings that would teach your children the truths about Jesus. Also note the books your kids particularly like. A special book purchased every so often that they picked out will surely become a favorite and an heirloom. And just think what it can accomplish in your child's heart!

5. Ask others to pray.

Being a mom is the same as being in a battle. You're a warrior! And the battle for your child's heart is a spiritual one! So enlist the prayer support of any family members who are Christians. If your parents or your husband's parents are believers, personally ask them to commit to becoming prayer warriors on behalf of your children. Ask them to pray for each of your children every day. And if there aren't any prayer warriors in your family, enlist a godly older woman or your best friend to join you in battle. Storm the gates of heaven for the souls under your charge!

5

Train Your Children in God's Ways

*Train up a child
in the way he should go,
and when he is old
he will not depart from it.*

PROVERBS 22:6

I've shared before in my books about my friend, Judy-the-gardener, and her incredibly beautiful garden. Well, delight of delights, Judy (also known as Judy-the-artist) and I collaborated on a children's book entitled *God's Wisdom for Little Girls*.[1] We weren't surprised that everyone's favorite painting is Judy's "little girl" busily working away in a corner of Judy's actual garden. To guide girls and their character development, I wrote:

The garden of God's little girl—how grand!
It began with a dream, a prayer, and a plan.

Nothing this splendid just happens, we know:
It takes time and care for flowers to grow.

How did Judy's garden come to be so magnificent? Multiple words are rushing in as I search for an answer. Commitment. Hard work. Dedication. Attention. Diligence. Creativity. Time. And I can't leave out...love! And all of these qualities and attitudes of heart have been worked out day after day for years on end.

Judy's training efforts go something like this. Each day, in the early-morning stillness she faithfully feeds, tills, and waters the roses that gift-wrap her arbor. Then, with sharpened shears, she cuts away any unruly growth, prunes off all unnecessary shoots, and removes every dead blossom. Surgically, Judy (who also used to be Judy-the-nurse!) removes any and every thing that would hinder the growth and development of her roses.

Oh, but she's not done yet! Next is the training process. Judy mounts her ladder and wires and tacks down her rose vines, carefully directing and redirecting their growth. She works away at this until she gets the results she wants and sees the design and beauty she has in mind emerging. Judy knows that growing a garden— even a single plant in a garden—is work. But it's a labor of love. And work is required of anyone who wants something grand.

Are you with me, mom? Are you guessing where we're going in a section about training children for God...and for life? We are going straight to the heart of what it means to train our children in God's ways!

Growing a Child

God wrote *The Book* on raising children, and He has much to say on the subject of training them. To begin, He expects us to actively prepare our children for life. In Proverbs 22:6, God gives His command—"train up a child in the way he should go." He also gives His encouragement—"and when he is old he will not depart from it." As moms with a heavenly charge to "train" each child, two efforts are required:

✓ *Educate*—One definition of *train* is to "educate," or "give instruction." This incorporates all parts of true religious education. How does this education take place? Do we wait until our baby can sit, walk, or talk, until our child reaches a certain age? Do we wait until we spot some glimmer of desire in the child? Do we count on a Christian school to do it for us? Or do we wait until our child gets into the Sunday-school system or the youth group at church?

✓ *Initiate*—This next definition answers these questions: To train also means to "initiate." You see, we as the parents must do the training and the educating. And we must be aggressive and take the initiative. Our training should be willful and on purpose, something we commit to, schedule, plan, and do, taking every opportunity to

educate our child "in the way he should
go."

And what happens if we don't initiate and educate our
children in the way they should go? They will go in the
way they want to go! Children left to choose their own
direction will be spoiled and self-centered in later life.
And the book of Proverbs teaches us "a child left to himself brings shame to his mother" (Proverbs 29:15).

Proverbs 22:6 (train up a child...) is also a warning
from God to parents: If we fail to train up our child, or
allow a child to train himself according to his own
wishes, we should not expect that child to want to
change this pattern in later life. That's because "children
are born sinners and, when allowed to follow their own
wishes, will naturally develop sinful habit responses....
Such habit patterns become deep-seated when they have
been ingrained in the child from the earliest days."[2]

Mom, realize you're on a mission to train up your children from the earliest minute possible. This training is
accomplished in two ways that never change.

Hands-on training—Like Judy with gloves, shears,
and wire, you are to actively and aggressively instruct
your "young plants" by hands-on training. Yes, you teach
your children the Bible. And of course you're teaching
them the rules to live by and how to do necessary, practical tasks. But are you teaching them how to make wise
choices? It's one of your jobs as a mom. So, as hard as it
is, don't give in to your natural mom instincts and make
all the choices for your child (which is easy to do but

damaging in the long run). Instead train them and show them how to make good decisions (for the long run!).

Active training also involves training your children through correction, which includes discipline when necessary.[3] One source put it something like this: Education commences at the mother's knee. You have to not only train your children *at* your knee but also, on occasion, *over* your knee! It takes *both* knees to train up a child in the way he should go. (More on this in a minute.)

Live-it-out training—This nonactive training process involves providing training and instruction by modeling right behavior. It's much more personal...and much more difficult. It's walking the walk in addition to talking the talk! To me the most frightening "mom" verse in the Bible is Proverbs 23:26: "My son, give me your heart, and let your eyes observe my ways." As the saying goes, It is noble to train a child in the way he should go, but better still is to walk that way yourself. While studying in college to become a teacher, I was constantly told, "You teach little by what you say, but you teach most by what you are." And the same is true of you as a mom. Your children will follow your footsteps more easily and often than they will follow your advice!

> *Train up a child in the way he should go, and go that way yourself!*[4]

The apostle Paul told other Christians to "imitate me, just as I also imitate Christ" (1 Corinthians 11:1). He reminded them that "the things which you learned and received and heard and saw in me, these do" (Philippians 4:9). We, as moms after God's heart, should be able to issue these same charges to our family too. Our lives should be a "copybook" they can follow.

I was so touched by this poem that I forwarded it on to my daughters. The wording is for parents of little boys, but it applies to raising little girls too.

> A careful [mom] I ought to be,
> A little fellow follows me.
> I do not dare to go astray,
> For fear he'll go the selfsame way.
>
> Not once can I escape his eyes;
> Whate'er he sees me do he tries.
> Like me he says he's going to be,
> That little chap who follows me....
>
> I must remember as I go
> Through summer sun and winter snow,
> I'm molding for the years to be—
> That little chap who follows me.[5]

From a Seedling

When is the best time for a mom to begin to "train up [her] child in the way he should go"? Obviously sooner is better. Like gardening, if we can begin from the outset with each little seedling, the training usually goes more smoothly. Reformed pastor and preacher Henry Ward Beecher well observed, "It is not hard to make a child or a tree grow right if you train them when they're young, but to make them straighten out after you've allowed things to go wrong is not an easy matter."

I'm always amazed at moms (and grandmoms too) who come through an autographing line and share that they think it is too early to begin reading my children's books—or any children's books, and even the Bible!—to their children. Why, they explain, they're only 9 or 12 months old, 18 months old, 2 years old, 4 years old! I try to be a lady, and I hold myself back as I let them know that I fiercely believe that it's never too early to begin training up little ones. Never. (Remember little Samuel in the Bible? At around age three he was already separated from his mom and serving God in the temple.)

So, whatever ages your little seedlings are, start the reading, teaching, and instructing...now. Initiate the training and teach your heart out. No matter what they do or don't understand, they will sense your love and passion. They'll also become accustomed to your voice and to your teaching. Believe me, they pick up much more than you can imagine. Think about this...

During a recent Thanksgiving holiday, Jim and I stayed in the basement/playroom/guestroom at our daughter Katherine's home in New York. We knew Paul had just painted the room in anticipation of our arrival, so we were surprised to see some dirt smudges on one wall in our quarters. But as we took a closer look, we saw the pencil markings of dates and the names of Kath and Paul's children...and lines with recorded height measurements! This, of course, brought smiles to our hearts and faces.

But here's what's alarming. Many parents (Jim and me included) are faithful to record their child's growth and development on walls, doorjambs, or journals. But long before that child can physically stand up to be measured, massive growth has been going on mentally, spiritually, and morally in that little person. Some parents don't even measure their children's growth until after their third birthday. And yet, when it comes to a child's heart and soul, "let every father and mother realize that when their child is three years of age, they have done more than half they will ever do for its character."[7]

> *The kind of person your child is going to be, he is already becoming... and becoming quickly!*[6]

Which Way, Lord?

Thank goodness when God said "train up a child" He didn't leave us moms with a vague job assignment! He didn't leave us wondering or worrying about the direction and desired outcome of our training. No, He told us in Proverbs 22:6 exactly what our purpose and objective is—to "train up a child in the way he should go." The "way he should go" answers our heart cry, "Which way, Lord?"

God's way—What do you think the right way is? If you said "God's way," you're correct. Proverbs tells us "the way of the Lord" is "the way of life," "the way of wisdom," and "the way of righteousness." This is more ammunition for making sure we teach God's Word to our children. Then they will know His way! And (again!) that's our job, mom—to teach our children God's way, train them in God's way, and insist that they follow God's way. Proverbs 6 says the law of the mother and her instruction "are the way of life" (verses 20-23).

I have taught you in the way of wisdom; I have led you in right paths.

PROVERBS 4:11

So instruct your heart out, dear mom! Live out God's way continually, teach God's Word constantly (Deuteronomy 6:7-8), and enforce God's wisdom consistently with loving discipline throughout your child's upbringing (Ephesians 6:4).

God's wisdom—Did I say "discipline"? Yes. Actually, God said it. And as moms after God's heart we do what He says. He says we are to teach our children, so we do. And He says we are to train our children, so we do. And part of that training involves His commands to correct and discipline our children, so we do.

> Discipline the child in whom you delight (Proverbs 3:12).
>
> Discipline while there is hope (19:18).
>
> Discipline diligently the child you love (13:24).
>
> Discipline a child in the way he should go (22:6).

>Discipline foolishness out of your child's heart (22:15).

>Discipline evil out of your child's heart (20:30).

Clearly the Bible teaches that to love your child is to discipline your child. Proverbs 13:24 states "he who spares his rod hates his son, but he who loves him disciplines him promptly." And Ephesians 6:4 cautions, "Do not provoke your children to wrath, but bring them up in the training and admonition of the Lord."

Oh did correcting and disciplining my two toddlers—my precious, darling little girls—ever come hard for me! In my book *A Woman After God's Own Heart*, I describe how I first heard this teaching from the Bible. How I didn't believe the teacher who taught it...until I read it in the Bible for myself. How I fought this truth, cried over it, and prayed through it. How I talked it over and hashed it through with Jim until we reached a mutual plan for implementing this wisdom from God. And then, how we dove into training up our little loved ones in the way they *should* go...not the way they *would*—and already were at such tender ages—go!

Those were hard days...and years! And if you need help getting started with biblical discipline—or encouragement to keep on or a fresh reminder to stay faithful—I've dedicated the entire "Little Things" section to a few "little" basics.

The child's way—Properly training up a child is a two-edged sword. On the one side, you must point them to God's way. And on the other, to enjoy any success at all in training your child for God and for life, you have to know your child, to know what makes him or her tick.

That's another message from God to His moms in Proverbs 22:6. This verse has been translated "educate a child according to his life requirements," "train a child for his proper trade,"[8] and point him in "the way"—his way, "that way selected for him in which he should go"[9]

In other words, each and every child is fearfully and wonderfully made and has his own "bent." There is a way or direction each is meant to grow and go in. Each of your little—and big!—ones has natural talents and personality traits that must be encouraged. For instance, maybe, like me trying to raise children who were only 13 months apart in age, you are trying to raise all of your children alike and train them all in the same way, with the same methods, and in the same direction.

And yet your children are individuals. For example, one of my girls is right-handed and the other a lefty. One is blessed to be a neatnick and the other is "a free spirit." One could be moved to tears of remorse by a stern or displeased look...and the other required stiffer consequences...again and again and again! Today both of these wonderful, unique, grown-up individuals and women of God love the Lord (and Jim and me!) and are moms themselves, but one is more on the artsy-craftsy, designer side and the other enjoys organizing and accounting.

My experience is just a thumbnail sketch with a few differences in "bent," but I'm sure you get the point. Your children are individuals with special strengths and capabilities—their own bent—that should be developed. God asks you to join with Him in the adventure and help them each discover, choose, and walk in the right path.

Harvesting the Fruit of Your Labors... and Love

At last we come to the hope of the fruit we may well reap in time—"Train up a child in the way he should go, and *when he is old he will not depart from it.*" Of course, there are exceptions to this "promise," but it still stands as a general rule. This favorite verse of Christian parents is not making an ironclad guarantee. But it is laying down a general principle. It's like this—just as a tree grows to be straight and healthy with a gardener's help (help like Judy gave her roses), so a child grows in the direction in which they are trained at home.

> *Tis education forms the infant mind; Just as the twig is bent, the tree's inclined.*[10]

And, yes, children raised in the nurture and admonition of the Lord can stray from God. But they can never get away from the prayers of their mom watering the seeds of God's Word and love that have been planted in their hearts through a lifetime. Chances are high that the seeds of faithful instruction will one day burst forth into life. The Scriptures, learned by heart, will move lost loved ones to remember their father's house, come to their senses, and return home (Luke 15:11-20).

Do you know what I want for you? It's the same thing I want for me. I want us to reap the harvest God is pointing to here in Proverbs 22:6. I want our children to "rise up"—to go out into public and go on with their lives as full-grown adults—and "bless" you, not verbally but by their lives (Proverbs 31:28). I want our children to be the next generation God and Moses were so concerned about in Deuteronomy 6. I want them to carry the baton of faith in God to yet another generation as they too train up their children in the way they should go.

Our chapter is running long, and part of the reason is because being a mom is one of my "hot buttons." I want you to take God's command to train up your children to heart. But I also want you to take heart, dear mom. How I wish I were right there with you. To listen. To share. To encourage. To rejoice...or to sorrow. To hug. To pray. But after all of the camaraderie and after the tissues are put away, I would tell you this....

Please, roll up your mothering sleeves and dive in. Give being a mom your heart, your all, your best, your time, your blood, sweat, and tears...and above all, your prayers! Learn all you can. Do all you can. Hang in there. Don't get discouraged. Don't even think about giving up. And pray always!

God has entrusted you with a new generation. And He's also given you all of the grace and strength and power and wisdom and love you will need for every step and second along the way. Believe it and own it. Never forget—you are a mom after God's heart. For this you were born.

From a Dad's Heart

As I just read this chapter in preparation for my "From Dad" section, I couldn't help but think back on something I wrote to teen guys in my book *A Young Man After God's Own Heart*.[11] I compared the training of soldiers at "boot camp" with the training of young men at home. Here's what I said in the chapter called "Training at Camp Home." (And by the way, this would apply to young girls as well.)

> Your home is God's training ground for your future. Train well, and you will have the tools and will develop the skills for a productive and influential life. Fail in your training at Camp Home, and the possibility of a lifetime of failure is greatly magnified.

Now, what should be of interest to you is that authentic training at military boot camp requires not only a willing recruit, but also a combat-hardened veteran drill sergeant for the training to be successful. (Do you see where I'm going with this analogy?) Your young recruits, whatever their ages, may or may not be willing, but that doesn't matter. God is asking you to do your part by becoming His "drill sergeant" in the home. He's asking you to take your young recruits and give them instruction for life and living, "to train them in the way they should go." Their future is partially dependent on how well you do your job at "Camp Home."

If your children are even as old as two or three, you probably already feel like a drill sergeant. All day long you are barking orders, giving instructions, inspecting bunks, and moving the troops from Point A to Point B. And in the evenings you try to hand off the responsibility to the master drill sergeant over your family, your husband, also known as Dad.

It's great when the "transfer of power" is successful and Drill Sergeant Dad takes over with the orders and the discipline. But, unfortunately, the ball gets dropped by Dad at times. Or, for whatever reason, he doesn't want the ball. Or he's away on business and not there for the hand off. What do you do then?

Whatever you do, don't go AWOL (Absent Without Leave)! Continue to stay at your post. Continue to carry out your orders and fulfill your duties. Ask God (your Commander-in-Chief) to sustain you in your role of trainer and drill sergeant. And pray for reinforcements!

And what if you're a single parent and there is no other drill sergeant? Then look to your church or family for reinforcements. Ask other godly men to be on call for those occasions when a man might help out, especially with training your boys. I do this for my daughter Courtney when her Navy husband is out to sea. One day she called and asked, "Dad, can you come over and talk to Jacob? He just needs a man in his life." Whom has God provided to assist you?

Little Choices That Reap Big Blessings

1. Start today!

It's never too early to start training your children. And it's also never too late. So whatever you do, do something today. Present neglect leads to later risk. And present neglect can also lead to future regret. It's easy to begin our work as a mother too late, but we can never begin it too soon. I once heard a godly dad share that his goal was to discipline his children so early in life that they not only got the message of right and wrong early on, but they also never remembered being disciplined!

2. Talk to your husband.

Seek to agree with your husband on the manner and methods you as a team will use for discipline and correction. Consistency is the goal. It's good for the parents, and it's good for the kids. It creates less confusion in your children...and sends them a loud, solid, unified message not to play one of you against the other.

3. Enroll in a parenting class at church.

When our girls were two and three, Jim and I took an invaluable class (it was only four sessions!)

on biblical child-raising taught by one of our church elders and his wife. We followed many of their principles for almost 20 years, until our daughters married. Coming from the Bible, their advice stood the test of time. Don't miss out on the wisdom that's available in your church. And if scheduling and classroom time is a problem, check out a parenting video or DVD from your church library. Just be sure you are growing in this sometimes perplexing part of life.

4. Be flexible.

Every minute of every day of every week of every year, your children change. So plan to review and adjust your child-raising regularly—at least weekly. Changes will always have to be made. *Always!* Constantly evaluate your training and discipline. What's working? What's not? What forms of discipline can be dropped? Which should be intensified or kicked up a notch?

5. Be generous with praise and encouragement.

Speak up when you see godly behavior in your children. When positive changes are made, praise God...and then praise your children. Let them know that you noticed. Celebrate! Brag on them. Tell dad what great things they have done. This is a terrific way to balance discipline with love.

Martin Luther, whose father was very strict, once wrote: "Spare the rod and spoil the child—that is true. But beside the rod keep an apple to give him when he has done well." Check yourself, mom. Do you encourage and praise at least as often as you reprove or correct?[12]

6. Pray like you've never prayed before!

We'll have an entire chapter on this "little choice" that reaps big blessing, but start praying now. Don't wait another second. These are *your* children! No one (other than God Himself) wants them to walk in God's ways more than you do. You'll need strength, wisdom, obedience, love—and lots of patience!—and these all come from God. So ask!

7. Have lots of fun!

One of my principles for being a mom was "Have a ball!" Training takes time, effort, and planning. And so does having fun. So create a page for every day this next week and plan in one element of fun. Let the party begin!

Ten Commands for Guiding Your Children

♡ Teach them, using God's Word
    (Deuteronomy 6:4-9).

♡ Tell them what's right and wrong
    (1 Kings 1:6).

♡ See them as gifts from God
    (Psalm 127:3).

♡ Guide them in godly ways
    (Proverbs 22:6).

♡ Discipline them (Proverbs 29:17).

♡ Love them unconditionally
    (Luke 15:11-32).

♡ Do not provoke them to wrath
    (Ephesians 6:4).

♡ Earn their respect by example
    (1 Timothy 3:4).

♡ Provide for their physical needs
    (1 Timothy 5:8).

♡ Pass your faith along to them
    (2 Timothy 1:5).[13]

$\mathscr{S}$usannah's Rules for $\mathscr{R}$earing Children

Can't think of any guidelines for your children? Let Susannah Wesley get you started. As the mother of 19 children, this noble mother developed these guidelines. Though 200-plus years old, her rules for teaching a child to be obedient are still helpful today.

1. Allow no eating between meals.

2. Put all children in bed by eight o'clock.

3. Require them to take medicine without complaining.

4. Subdue self-will in a child and thus work together with God to save his soul.

5. Teach each one to pray as soon as he can speak.

6. Require all to be still during family worship.

7. Give them nothing that they cry for, and only that which they ask for politely.

8. To prevent lying, punish no fault which is first confessed and repented of.

9. Never allow a sinful act to go unpunished.

10. Never punish a child twice for a single offense.

11. Commend and reward good behavior.

12. Any attempt to please, even if poorly performed, should be commended.

13. Preserve property rights, even in the smallest matters.

14. Strictly observe all promises.

15. Require no daughter to work before she can read well.

16. Teach children to fear the rod.[14]

6

$\mathcal{T}$ake Care of Your Children

*If a son asks for bread
from any father among you
will he give him a stone?*

LUKE 11:11

y good friend Lisa is known as "Dr. Tatlock" to her students at The Master's College where she teaches home economics. In the book she authored with Dr. Pat Ennis, *Designing a Lifestyle that Pleases God,* Lisa shares about "the culture shock of motherhood" and her struggle to adjust to her role as a new mom. (Sound familiar? Bring back any memories?) To help make the transition from being a professional with a doctoral degree to mommy-hood, Lisa made this list in an attempt to keep her sense of humor.

127

You Know You're a Mommy When...

"Sleeping late" on a Saturday morning is 7 A.M.!

You get up on Sunday mornings at 5:30 A.M. and are still late for church!

You know the location of every drive-through bank, pharmacy, and restaurant (so you don't have to do the car-seat-to-stroller/stroller-to-car-seat workout routine on every errand)!

The grocery store is an exciting family outing!

Weekly menu plans and recipes come from the *20 Minutes or Less* cookbook!

You have your "quiet times" with the Lord during the 2 A.M. baby feeding!

Macaroni-and-cheese or peanut butter-and-jelly sandwiches become your lunch delicacies!

You discover you really can talk on the phone, give the baby his bottle, and play cars with your toddler all at once!

You used to need an hour to get ready to go out but now are excited about having ten uninterrupted minutes to fix your hair and change your clothes!

Staying up late is 9 P.M.![1]

I love it! Lisa's list illustrates the amount of time, effort, and love involved in taking care of your children. If you were to make your own "you know you're a mommy when" list, I'm sure it would point to this same common denominator: We love our children by taking care of them. It's a more-than-full-time job...beginning with food! (Did you notice five of Lisa's ten mommyisms dealt with food?)

What's for Dinner?

Some say love is spelled t-i-m-e, but just maybe it's spelled f-o-o-d. How many times have your kids of all ages (and their dad too!) come in and asked in whatever vocabulary they have, "What's for dinner? When's dinner? Eat?" Mealtime is a fact of life. No matter when you made the last meal, it's already time for the next one! I know as a mom with a thriving, growing family, I had to face this daily fact head on. Just because I wasn't hungry didn't mean my little ones weren't. And just because I was in a time squeeze didn't mean time could be squeezed out of mealtimes.

Luckily, the Proverbs 31 mom in the Bible showed me how to take care of my family's food needs. From her I learned a mom "watches over the ways of her household," including the Food Department (verse 27). She also taught me that to put food in front of a family often means a mom "rises while it is yet night, and provides food for her household" (verse 15). In other words, food for my family was to be a top priority each day, and I needed to do whatever it took to obtain it, fix it, and serve it each day.

As I began spending the time and effort required to feed my family, I discovered two main benefits that made a super impact on both them and me.

Tiger's milk—First, nutrition is the key to growth and development. I began to think of myself as serving up "Tiger's Milk"[2] to my cubs—food that promoted their good health. The body of every person, even an unborn child, thrives on nutrients and minerals. That's why we moms put on yet another hat and study nutrition. We become experts on what's best for our family's health and how to maintain each · person's ideal weight.

> *Feed me with the food that is needful for me.*
>
> PROVERBS 30:8[3]

Get-up-and-go power—Next, energy. You know that eating the right foods shoots both quick and sustaining energy through your system. Food is jet fuel to the body. We see this in the story about Jonathan, the son of King Saul (1 Samuel 14:24-32). Saul gave a rash order that the people under his command could not eat. Obviously the longer they went without food, the weaker and more downhearted they became. But Jonathan, unaware of the command, touched the point of a stick into a honeycomb. When he tasted the honey, his eyes brightened, and he was refreshed and energized. Sadly, the people's need for food was so great they ate what God had forbidden.

As moms with a heart for doing the right thing for our family unit, we feed them the right things and at regular intervals. This boosts blood sugar and protein levels, creating a higher level of sustained energy...no matter how big or little a person is.

Give us this day our daily bread.

Matthew 6:11

As I grew as a mom, TLC— Tender Loving Care—took on new meaning. I went to work learning what it took to fuel my family. I learned to plan ahead for meals and snacks. I learned to make a weekly menu every Sunday afternoon. I learned to make a schedule for each day that included all meals and snack times. And I learned to back that schedule up and factor in prep time.

How are you doing in this vital area? I know you're busy. I know there's a permanent dust cloud behind your car as you race here and there to fulfill all your responsibilities. But if you wrote down what you served your brood during the past seven days, what would it reveal? Our goal as moms is to see that those in our family are not deprived of the food, nutrition, health, and energy they need to handle daily life, prevent melt-downs, and stay happy.

And don't forget to balance out the nutritionally correct foods with a few family favorites. Do you know each child's three favorite foods? And are they on hand for special times? (And why am I thinking about pizza!)

And another don't forget: Eat together! It's the secret to food in any family. I recently read a list of 50 ways to love your children, and one of them was to "eat meals together." It was followed by 25 ways to enjoy your family, one being "eat dinner together as a family for seven days in a row."[4]

Will I Be Safe Today?

Are you surprised to learn that of the 12 things kids of all ages worry about every day, "Will I be safe today?" ranks near the top?[5] I was! But as I researched the Proverbs 31 woman for my book *Beautiful in God's Eyes,*[6] I discovered that many of the descriptive Hebrew images of her care for her family pictured her as a lioness tending and watching over her cubs. She not only fed her babies, she also protected them...fiercely! Let's take this imagery into our homes. How can we fiercely protect our cub-children? At home they need...

Protection from siblings—Home is a shelter for every family member. Teach your children that home is where peace reigns. Sure, you can have fun and engage in friendly roughhousing. And joyful laughter is the rule of the day. But don't let things get out of control. And make sure your kids don't hurt or harass or threaten their brothers and sisters.

Protection from accidents—Do your best to set up and reinforce safety practices. It's an ongoing job, but teach your children to put away toys, both inside and outside, to prevent falls, scrapes, and broken bones. Tuck electric cords out of harm's way and cover empty sockets. Childproof your drawers and cupboards with safety latches to protect little inquisitive people and happy wanderers. Establish rules—with consequences for violators—for going into the street, for bike-riding without a helmet, and so forth. Have an "everyone buckles-up!" seatbelt policy.

Protection from incidents—Do your children know their name, address, and phone number, and what to do if they get lost? (Our granddaughter, Taylor, as a toddler in New York City, learned this information right along with the lyrics to "Jesus Loves Me" and the alphabet song. It was a must!) Do your kids know to dial 911 for help? Do they know what to do, say, or not say when approached by strangers?

Deliver us from evil.

MATTHEW 6:13 KJV

Protection through education— Much protection of our children is accomplished by faithful instruction. Another of our mom assignments is instructing each child about the dangers of being in the wrong places or with the wrong crowd, about talking to strangers, about sexual purity.

The first time I read the book of Proverbs, I couldn't believe it. The writer of this book of wisdom—a father—addressed "my son" at least 21 times! His advice spells out the "how-to" and "do not" instructions we must give our kids to protect them. This passionate parent pleaded,

"My son, if sinners entice you, do not consent." "My son...the lips of an immoral woman drip honey....Hear me now, my children...remove your way far from her, and do not go near the door of her house." "My son...keep my words...that they may keep you from the immoral woman....Listen to me, my children...do not let your heart turn aside to her ways."[7]

We learn a valuable parenting lesson from this concerned dad and writer of biblical wisdom. His instruction for his son and children was

> from the heart,
> to the point, and
> filled with specifics.

He gave explicit details and clear instructions. This dad wanted his son to know *exactly* how a prostitute or loose woman dressed, talked, and acted. And he wanted his son to know *exactly* what happens to the one who falls under her spell. And he wanted his son to know *exactly* what to do to avoid temptation and destruction.

Protection from the internet—This new front requires a parent's protection. Our kids need our serious instruction and involvement. I still grieve with the mom whose little boy viewed pornography on an educational internet hookup at school. It seems another second grader wanted to show everyone what he could do online. The bottom line is, We can't think this couldn't happen to our children. It could even happen right in our own homes! So we need to aggressively do our part and take precautions. What can we do? Purchase a computer program that restricts risky websites and dubious infiltrators. Set up a super-thick parental firewall with multiple restrictions, blocks, passwords, and filters. Make a rule that a parent must be present for any school-aged child to use the internet. Keep the home computer in the family room where we can monitor activity. Limit the number of minutes and set a cut-off time for each family member's online time. Regularly look over the file names of the sites our kids are visiting.

I will set nothing wicked before my eyes.

PSALM 101:3

Protection from TV—TV can become another violator of our children's mental health and moral purity. So again we go to battle. Block questionable channels. Stand strong against the trend of putting a TV in each child's room; have everyone watch TV in the family room. We can also set limits on TV time and programs.

Be careful, little eyes, what you see; be careful, little ears, what you hear.

I recently heard a CD by a dad who limited his children to one hour of TV a week. He sat with them while they watched what they selected and he approved. Afterward, they followed up by talking about the program. He finished his story saying today, as adults, his children have TVs that they seldom watch. During the years of limited TV, they learned to spend their time and minds on much more interesting activities.

Protection from the opposite sex—Have you noticed the progression in this chapter from the dailies of food and safety at home to the biggie—to sex? The faithful watchcare over our flocks stretches far beyond putting meals on the table. Yes, we moms take care of our children's physical well-being, but we also keep an eye out for their sexual and moral well-being. No scar is as deep and as permanent as the loss of sexual purity.

Several of our topics have already addressed this big area in children's lives, an area which calls for high-gear parental involvement. We must never forget we are in a serious battle for the purity of our children. True, we live in the world, but we don't have to succumb to its lures, temptations, and lack of standards.

"*Flee sexual immorality*" and "*glorify God in your body.*"

1 Corinthians 6:18,20

As a member of God's brigade of moms, set the highest standards for your children. (I mean, as high as the heavens! As high as God's Word!) Work relentlessly at communicating those standards clearly. Enforce them sternly, and hold any and all lines. If ever there was a place for you to get tough, to be passionate and fierce, this is it. Your kids need to know their purity is 100 percent important to God, 100 percent important to you, and it should be 100 percent important to them too.

Fellow mom, share your heart earnestly. Don't be afraid to be thought of as strict or prudish, or old-fashioned. You can take it! Regardless of what happens, you'll be glad to know that you did all you could. That you spoke up. That you cared.

Keep your growing kids in the Bible, and keep on having devotions at home. Take them to church. Help them develop relationships with solid believers, peers, mentors, and youth leaders at church. Talk openly and regularly about the details of their daily lives, about their standards and their relationships. Let them know you love them and care about them. And above all else, keep on praying!

Why Do I Have to Rest?

Do you wish someone would make you take a nap? While we tend to function on sleep-deprivation mode, each of our little ones needs to rest, yet constantly asks, "Why do I need to rest?" Everyone gets tired, run down, and stressed out. And if time out for rest isn't taken, prepare for a complete meltdown! Lack of sleep robs everyone of the rest needed for health, for coping, for energy, for clear thinking. Even Jesus, in His humanity, was weary (John 4:6). He also understood His disciples' need for rest and initiated a time of R & R for them (Mark 6:31).

So we, like Jesus, look out for the rest needed by our "disciples" at home. For the baby, sleep is essential for growth and development. That means we moms need to create schedules that factor in that needed sleep time. For preschoolers, it's a full out tug-of-war! That means we need to be the boss, to assert ourselves, and ensure that whether they sleep or not during nap time, they at least get some rest and a little down time. For school-aged family members, adequate rest comes down to getting them into bed good and early.

For older kids with homework, commitments, and jobs—and, of course, lots of friends!—we definitely enter into a whole new scene. In their case, we watch out and watch over what keeps them up at night. (Remember the woman from Proverbs 31 who watches over her household? That's you, mom!) What—and who—are the culprits? Phone calls? The internet, email, or text messaging with friends? TV programs? Caffeine? Sugar? For everyone's sake, especially your teen's, be firm. Set house rules. Go to work on eliminating or curtailing whatever is interfering with them getting their homework done and getting to bed.

Obviously there's more—much more!—to taking care of your children than these few pages allow me to highlight. And more will be addressed in the "Little Choices" that follow. But in this section we're dealing with the heart of a mom after God's own heart. It's true, we may not get too excited about running our home on a schedule or cooking another meal or doing another load of laundry or being on parental patrol duty. But a heart filled with motherly love does all of the above.

And what if you are a working-outside-the-home mom? Taking care of your children is just as important but even more difficult. And you know why, don't you. Because you're not with your children as much as you would like, and they are under the care of others part of the time. Some caregivers have your same convictions and standards, but unfortunately many don't. This means you'll have to redouble your efforts when you are with your children to ensure that when they are away from you, they still have your standards, which are God's standards.

And what if your older kids are home alone for a time before you or your husband arrive? Again, you'll need to really impress upon them what the boundaries and standards are at home—and what the consequences are for not following the house rules.

Dear mom, I know the things covered in this chapter are your heart concerns too. I probably haven't brought up anything you didn't already know. My intention has been a little like the apostle Peter's role in his letters. He saw himself as a *reminder*. He wrote his readers that he would "not be negligent to *remind* you always of these things, though you know and are established in the present truth." He desired "to stir up by reminding" (2 Peter 1:12-13).

I'm not in any way suggesting that you're not doing your best. What I am doing is reminding you (and me too!) of God's privileged calling to take care of your children...in the best way you know how, with as much zeal as you can gain from the Lord, for as long as you have the opportunity.

From a Dad's Heart

"How many children do you have?" I'll bet you've been asked that hundreds of times. You think for a minute and reply in jest, "I have three children. Two boys, ages 6 and 10, and one aged 35." Sometimes that's half true. I don't know what it is with us guys when it comes to our families. We are dynamos at work. We can keep three secretaries busy all day, move ten men forward on a construction site, provide service for others all day and into the night.... But when it comes to our kids, we can be clueless!

As one who was raised in a home with a hard-working, unbelieving father who didn't provide a lot of modeling in the Care Department, let me give you a few suggestions on how to help your husband in this area.

1. Consider yourself blessed by God if you have a husband who helps care for the children at all. He is a rare breed! Be sure to thank him.

2. If your husband isn't as concerned as you are, don't see it as a character flaw. See it more as an educational flaw. Elizabeth steadily

encouraged me in the direction of being a more caring father. How? See #4.

3. Make sure you are doing all *you* can to care for your children in the areas you are in charge of: nutrition, safety, hygiene, manners, sleep, playmates, daytime TV, to name a few.

4. Once you have evaluated your heart and your level of commitment, sit down with dad. Share your concerns for the children. Ask him what you, he, and both of you should do about your concerns. Ask for his input and suggestions. What does he see being done, not done, needing improvement?

5. Many areas of childcare are your responsibility. So it's important that you get a report card of how well you are doing. Who better to ask than your husband and the children's dad? He sees you day in and day out. Ask for his evaluation. And don't react if he gives you a little constructive criticism. Respond positively. Thank him for his observations and suggestions. Then go to God and prayerfully evaluate his comments. Take them as coming from the Lord and act on them. Then later on, ask for another progress report!

6. Enlist and encourage your husband's support and leadership, especially as the children get a little older. Let him be the point man regarding school friends, school curriculum, relationships with the opposite sex, dating standards, curfews, house rules.

7. Ask your husband to read Job 1:4-5 with you. Job was concerned for the spiritual condition of his adult children. He prayed and offered sacrifices for them just in case they had offended God. That's the model of daily care and concern God is asking of you and your husband. Together, make a covenant to pray for your children, whether they are one or twenty-one. God sees your care starting when those children are conceived, and He desires that you continue that care as long as you can, even if it's just to pray for your long-gone-from-home adult children.

Little Choices That Reap Big Blessings

1. Bone up on diet and nutrition.

(And I don't mean a weight-loss diet...unless one is needed!) Diet means "a way of life." Every mom, including you, can always learn more about diet and nutrition. After all, you're the head of that department. So go online or to the bookstore and bone up. Discover how you can improve the health of your loved ones.

2. Eat dinner together tonight.

If it's possible, gather everyone together—at the same time. (That may count as a miracle!) What will you serve? When will you eat? And where? How can you jazz up the table a bit? And what can you do to make the meal special, whimsical, fun, a time of sharing? Then work on one of the suggestions in this chapter—plan to eat dinner together seven days in a row.

3. P.E. anyone?

Physical Education class was always a welcomed break in a long school day, wasn't it? So factor in physical activities for your restless—or sedentary—ones. Keep the kids physically active. What can they do outside? Is there a park nearby? A walking path? A sprinkler on a hot summer day? Be creative. Make sure your kids get lots of exercise. And, amazingly, if the TV is off, children always find something to do and usually end up outside...playing. The exertion increases health, helps guard against weight gain, and burns up excess energy in your young ones.

4. Limit TV time.

There's no doubt the TV can be mom's helper when it's crunch time—you know, between four and five in the afternoon. But just for today, set a limit on the time and times the TV will be on.

After a few days of limited viewing as a break-in time, design a workable plan for the household. What are the best programs for your children to watch? And which ones are absolutely out? What is each child's favorite program? How many minutes a day should the kids spend in front of the TV? And consider this: I read about one family that selected three nights per week they would not even turn the TV on.

And don't forget to follow-up on something most important: Find the instructions for how to block or remove certain channels on your TV. Don't know where they are? They're available online through your TV's brand name.

5. Establish a daily routine.

Everyone—including moms—are more productive and feel better about their lives when they have a consistent daily routine. It's called "horizontal planning"—trying to do the same thing at the same time each day.

Children do better with a routine too. They thrive on knowing what's next, knowing what to expect. It gives them confidence and a sense of order. Establish a schedule for your family for Monday through Friday. (Saturday and Sunday are always another story!) There will be less tension and confusion, and attitudes and productivity will improve, both at home and at school.

6. Double-check reasons behind misbehavior.

Are the kids acting up, talking back, grumpy, and requiring additional discipline? Are they getting the basics of nutritious, scheduled meals, and adequate sleep and rest? Check out what's not going on at home to make sure you're doing all you can do in providing for their needs.

7. Factor in some fun.

Where does family fun come from? Out of mom's happy heart. This book is about ways to love your children. Don't forget to plan in some fun time with your children every day.

8. Enjoy Proverbs 31:10-31.

Plan a special break in your mommy madness, set out your favorite drink, curl up, and read through this poem. Notice the ways this mom who, just like you, took care of her children. You'll be encouraged in your role of being a mom after God's own heart!

7

Take Your Children to Church

*Let the little children come to Me,
and do not forbid them.*

MARK 10:14

Good things happen to the family that goes to church—good things that pay dividends for generations and generations. Do you believe it? It's hard to imagine—and understand—what attending church can mean eternity wise. Sundays are just a small commitment of a tiny slice of time each week, yet this one little practice, slowly, steadily, and surely, over time, supernaturally ingrains something into a soul. Sooner or later it makes a difference in a life, a heart, and in a family.

I know that's certainly been true for our family. And it all began with parents who were faithful to take Jim and me to church when we were growing up. I only share our stories to point out how this one activity on our parents' parts paid the highest dividends—that is, eternal dividends—in each of our lives years and years down the line, extending now to two more generations.

One Little Girl

In my case, my parents took me and my three brothers to church every Sunday. I don't remember ever not liking to go or not wanting to go. I mean, it was *somewhere* to go! And that's always appealing to a child, even (and maybe especially!) to a teen. I personally couldn't get enough of church. I loved my teachers there, and my youth leaders who came later on. I enjoyed participating in all of the activities and gatherings, including the youth choir. The more the better! And I looked forward to summer church camp all year long.

> *Please take me to Sunday school and church regularly... I enjoy learning more about God.*[1]

A child's heart is tender and receptive to spiritual truths and experiences, and mine was no different. As a little one with petticoated dresses, black patent leather shoes, and bows in clean curled hair, I looked forward to sitting around the little low tables with kid-sized matching chairs and hearing another story about Jesus, followed up by working on activities and projects, coloring lesson papers, and singing. I loved learning about God and Jesus and heroes like Joshua (and the walls that fell down!) and David (killing the awful giant with a mere rock in a slingshot!). And I still recall my teen years and how I loved to pray. I hung out in my room and journaled about my love for God. I wrote out my prayers. And I loved going to each and every activity for my age group, where there were caring people and friendships formed in small groups.

As you'll see in a second, I didn't become a Christian during those going-to-church-years. But, praise God, seeds were sown and watered!

One Little Boy

Jim too grew up going to church several times a week. As he's already shared, in his family only he (an only child) and his mother (a true mom after God's own heart!) went. Like every little boy, Jim couldn't wait to get out of the house and go somewhere—anywhere! His Sunday school teachers were like part of his family. And at church he participated in a Bible club where he memorized 600 Bible verses and won the highest possible award. (That's always good for any kid. Just think of the lessons learned. The discipline. The thrill of achievement. And the priceless, eternal, living Word of God in a tender young heart!)

The Difference Church Can Make

I must tell you that when both Jim and I left our childhood homes to go to college, neither of us continued to go to church. And when we met on campus, fell in love, and married, Jim was a Christian and I was not.

As a newly formed family unit, we thought, What a good time to begin going to church again! So we attended church...exactly two times—the first two Sundays after our wedding. We went exactly once to Jim's childhood church denomination and once to mine. But because we couldn't agree on either, we never went to any church again...

...until our two little girls were one and two years old. And then, because church had been a part of our childhood years, Jim and I wanted to provide the same experience for our little ones. (You understand, *they* needed it, right?) So we started taking Katherine and Courtney to church. It was quite an adventure as we turned again and again to the phone book and selected churches to visit...until we found one we all liked.

Oh, dear reading friend! There isn't space for sharing the details. It would be a very poor attempt at trying to describe the by-God's-grace-transformation that the "little choice" to go to church launched in our family. But, please,

> *Putting God first puts a powerful example before our children.*

let me just state this: In both Jim and me, God used our parents' dedication to taking us to church ...to cause us to want to go to church...to cause us to want to take our children to church... where I became a Christian and Jim renewed His commitment to Christ.

And then what happened? You guessed it! In time, our little

ones became believers in Christ...and they are now taking *their* little ones to church.

Jesus and Church

According to the Bible, our Savior was "taken to church" (so to speak) by Mary and Joseph, a set of righteous parents who sought to keep God's law. In Luke 2:41-42 we learn that Jesus' "parents went to Jerusalem every year at the Feast of the Passover. And, when [Jesus] was twelve years old, they went up to Jerusalem according to the custom of the feast."

Jesus, of course, was the fullness of God and the perfect Son of God, so our focus right now is not on Him, but on His parents. The Bible says His "parents went to Jerusalem every year at the Feast of Passover" (verse 41). We note here *their* faithfulness to take their child—even "that Holy One" (Luke 1:35)—to worship in Jerusalem. Why would they bother to make the strenuous journey from Nazareth to Jerusalem to attend the Passover? Because of their commitment and love for God, and because it was the right thing to do.

The Savior grew up in a home where God's laws were obeyed and the prescribed annual festivals were faithfully observed. In Jesus' family and culture, families worshiped together. There was no such thing as dropping your kids off at church and going out shopping or for brunch or coffee. No, the parents took the children to worship with them.

Why Is Church So Important?

As New Testament believers, we are not bound to the Old Testament law. However, the kind of love Joseph and Mary had for God as a man, a woman, a couple, and parents after God's own heart burns in our hearts too. And such a love for the Lord leads to following His instructions (John 14:15). The Bible urges us to "consider one another in order to stir up love and good works, not forsaking the assembling of ourselves together, as is the manner [or habit] of some, but exhorting one another, and so much the more as you see the Day [of the gathering together of the elect to Christ at His coming][2] approaching" (Hebrews 10:24-25).

What's so important about gathering together with other Christians at church? It strengthens us because of the like-mindedness of the faith of those present. As we come in out of the world and gather together with other believers, we grow in our faith in Christ and in our trust in God. We are bolstered and boosted in our Christianity. We receive encouragement and advice from others and strengthen them in the same way.

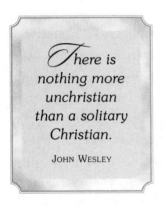

There is nothing more unchristian than a solitary Christian.

JOHN WESLEY

I began this chapter by stating "good things happen to a *family* that goes to church." But, mom, good things happen to *you* too. For instance, going to church...

> is an opportunity to hear the heart, mind, and voice of your pastor (Colossians 4:16).

is a time to join your heart with others in
unified worship (1 Timothy 2:8-12).

is a time to blend your voice together with
others in praise to God (Matthew 26:30;
Ephesians 5:19).

is a time to give sacrificially to the Lord
(1 Corinthians 16:2).

is an opportunity to have a shared experience with both young and old (Acts
2:42).[3]

No church is perfect, and going to church doesn't
make you a Christian. But as I've already said, it's a
supernatural experience and good things will happen
because of your obedience.

Jesus' Take on Children

Jesus-the-boy grew up to be revealed and recognized
as Jesus-the-Savior. And He too speaks of the importance
of children being exposed to Him, His life, and His
teachings. In one scene in the Bible, we witness parents
who were eager to bring their little ones to Jesus. Note
what happened in Mark 10:13-16:

> Then they brought little children to Him, that
> He might touch them; but the disciples
> rebuked those who brought them.

> But when Jesus saw it, He was greatly dis-
> pleased and said to them, "Let the little chil-
> dren come to Me, and do not forbid them;

for of such is the kingdom of God. Assuredly,
I say to you, whoever does not receive the
kingdom of God as a little child will by no
means enter it."

And He took them up in His arms, laid His
hands on them, and blessed them.

Do you wonder why Jesus rebuked His disciples who
thought it best to protect their Master from annoyances
and interruptions? It was because they erroneously
thought that babes and young ones were incapable of
receiving anything from Jesus. But they were wrong.
Besides holding and blessing the infants and toddlers,
Jesus used them as an exhortation to those present that
they must receive the kingdom of God with childlike
trust.

There's something else here in this sweet scene. It's a
strong admonition to parents too. "Jesus' words forcefully
confront parents and all those in contact with children:
Are we helping or hindering children from coming to
Christ? Are we, ourselves, receiving the kingdom of God
with childlike trust?"[4]

Are you, mom? Are you helping your children come to
know about Christ? Are you taking them to church regularly? Faithfully? I want to repeat Dr. George Barna's
survey results here: "People are much more likely to
accept Christ as their Savior when they are young.
Absorption of biblical information and principles typically
peaks during the preteen years."[5]

But What If...?

It's "But what if...?" time again. Amazingly, a little thing like going to church can become a big issue!

*What if...*my children don't want to go to church? First of all, pray! Then stand firm. You're the adult, the parent, the one God has given authority to train up your children for life and for Him. You're in charge. One book I read included a section that covered "the principle of relent-less parenting."[6] I like that. You're not a best friend or a buddy to your kids. There's a place for that, but you are primarily their parent. So hang in there. Don't coast, back down, or back out. Make the decisions and rules, and hold the line. And if you decide (along with your husband, of course) that your family is going to go to church, then your family is going to go to church.

*What if...*I'm a new Christian and my children are older and don't want to go to church? Again, pray! Then tell your family what's happened to you, about who Jesus is and what He's done for you. Let them know going to church will benefit everyone, including them, that it's been a missing element in your family, and you're sorry about that. Ask them to come along with you and see what's happening. And keep praying!

*What if...*due to a divorce, my children are with their other parent(s) on weekends and don't go to church? This time, pray, pray, *pray!* The time you do have with your kids is critical. Take time to nurture your heart and their hearts, teach them God's Word, talk to them about

God, tell them about Jesus, train them in God's ways. Be sure you prepare your kids for each time they'll be away from you. You must do your part, and then trust the Lord for them. He knows your situation. He knows your children's situation when they're away from you. And prepare to receive them back...and continue the loving and godly training.

Heart Response

"Take them to church." This one decision harvests positive fruit for a lifetime (and Lord willing, for eternity!) in the hearts and lives of our children. As we prepare to leave this tiniest and easiest of all commitments—that of simply taking our children to church—let's examine our mom hearts.

- ✓ How's my attendance and my zeal?— Church isn't the worst thing you have to do, but the best. It's your greatest privilege and something to look forward to all week. The psalmist declared, "I was glad when they said to me, 'Let us go into the house of the LORD'" (Psalm 122:1). Is this the attitude of your heart?

- ✓ How regularly are my children getting to church?—The story's been told that near a church in Kansas, the prints of two baby feet with the toes pointing toward the church are forever implanted in a cement sidewalk. It's said that scores of years ago, when the sidewalk was being laid, a mom after God's own heart who wanted her little boy to start out right, secured permission to stand her baby boy on the wet cement. The tracks are plainly seen today.[7] In what direction are your children's feet pointed?

✓ What's keeping my children from going to church?—Is it the time and effort it takes to get the family up, dressed, fed, and out the door a *sixth* day in your week? Is it late-night Saturdays? Is it other commitments your family's made for the Lord's Day? What part of this are you responsible for?

✓ Am I giving my children minimum or maximum exposure to church?—There is church...and then there is *church!* For instance, instead of one service for your children, most churches provide two services of teaching and activities for kids. As long as you're going to the trouble to prepare and get everyone to church, get twice the mileage out of your efforts. Stay as long as possible.

Go to the limit when it comes to church and your children. Ambassadors, Awana, Cubbies, Sparks Bible clubs?

> They'll be there! Church camp? They're
> going! Gym nights? Sign them up! Back-
> yard barbecues and get-togethers? Send
> along some hot dogs! Campfire times at
> the beach? Youth fellowship night? Sat-
> urday gatherings? There's no way they're
> missing out on spiritual growth opportuni-
> ties!

Dear busy mom, I went through this entire checklist—
and more!—as a going-to-church-beginner when my girls
were little. Our family knew what life was like without
church...and it wasn't all that good. In fact, it was empty.
Sunday mornings consisted of sticking our little ones in
front of the TV, sleeping in, reading the *Los Angeles Times*
for hours while sipping coffee in our pj's until the ball
games started on TV.

And oh do I ever remember the first time we set the
alarm clock(!) on Sunday morning. But the blessings!
They are countless, life-changing, and eternal. Going to
church focused us on good things that carried us into
and through the next week. It anchored our family on
biblical principles. It flavored the daily atmosphere at
home with the sweet aroma of Christ. It introduced us to
other Christian families and friends. It brought meaning
to the days of our lives. And it turned our feet, hearts,
and minds away from the things of this world and set our
affection on things above—on Christ.

I'm still thanking God daily for His gracious interven-
tion in our lives, for the Christian friends Jim and I have,
for the friends and teachers who positively influenced

our children, for the mates they met at church, and for our seven little grandchildren who are now toddling off to church to their classes and teachers and lessons about Jesus.

What a blessing it is for you and your family to be part of a greater family—the body of Christ, the family of God!

From a Dad's Heart

I have to say, when it comes to taking children to church, the mom is a key player. The dad can definitely help, but you, mom, are usually the one who sets and runs the schedule for Sunday and for pacing the week as it leads up to going to church. Because you live for Sunday and for seeing your family at church together, you plan for it all week long. By Sunday you have planned your meals, set out the clothes for the children, and tried to get everyone into bed early on Saturday night. And all of this with at least some help from your husband, I hope...which brings up a couple of "what ifs" that I want to cover.

What if...my husband doesn't want to go to church with us? I'm a resident expert on this one. As you know, my dad wasn't a Christian. But somehow my mother made his life so pleasant that he didn't mind her going to church and taking me along with her. Even during the summer, my mom and I drove 30 miles each way to go to church from our cabin on the lake where my dad liked us to go as a family every weekend. Then we were right back on that lake by one o'clock to fix lunch for my dad.

I'm sure my mother invited my dad to go with us, but I can't remember him ever going to church, except when his mother died. So, like my mom, be the best wife you can be. Your husband will see a correlation between your church involvement and your life at home and will more than likely gladly give you and those sweet children up for a few hours each week.

What if...my husband doesn't want me and the children to go to church? This is a difficult place to be in as a wife and mom. You know what church means to you and the kids, and it's unfortunate to have an antagonistic husband. First, check your own heart, and evaluate your conduct around your husband and at home. Is he upset with your *faith* or with *you?* Are you portraying a form of Christianity that's unbiblical? Is your husband feeling neglected? Does he see your church attendance as driving a wedge between him and you and the children?

Ask God to show you areas where you can better demonstrate Christ's love to your husband. Also ask your husband what bothers him about your going to church. Try to reassure him that church will help you become a better wife and mother and that his children will be better for it as well.

*What if...*you work on Sunday? This is sometimes unavoidable. But if taking your children to church is a priority, then you will want a schedule where you have time for church, even if it means a pay cut. God will honor your commitment and, Lord willing, your children will grow up with a love for God and the things of God, including going to church.

One of the greatest blessings of a parent is seeing your grown children following in your footsteps and making an effort to be regular at church. It's at these times that you thank God you made the effort to take them to church throughout their formative years.

Little Choices That Reap Big Blessings

1. Debrief Sunday school lessons.

My favorite part of going to church as a family is when the little ones run out of their Sunday school class waving their lesson paper in their hands. They can't wait to give it to their moms! Listen as your kids blurt out something on the run. Be sure in the fuss and flurry of visiting with others and getting to the car and home that you don't misplace this paper treasure!

Then make this one little choice when you get home: Sit down with your children individually and go over the story or activity featured in their lesson activities. Let them tell you the lesson... about Jesus healing blind eyes, about how the stone got rolled away from the tomb, about the handmade scroll with "all scripture is given by inspiration of God" copied on it. Don't miss the opportunity to reinforce these truths in young hearts. And with the older kids, tap on the door, plop on their beds, and ask what their teacher or youth pastor talked about today. Just listen. Punctuate often with, "That's good!...Oh, I like that!" What a blessing you receive as you hear firsthand

how God's Word is working in little—and big—
hearts!

2. Begin the night before.

Guard the evening before church. Consider
making it your "family night" at home. Begin
bath time early. Select and lay out church clothes
and Bibles. Set an early curfew for teens. Get the
kids to bed a little earlier than usual. (And don't
forget to make all these same little choices concerning yourself too. Things will go more
smoothly the next morning.) Then let the blessings begin!

3. Have a teacher's meeting.

How many parent–teacher meetings have you
had in your lifetime? If you have school-age
kids, probably a lot! So why not schedule a
meeting with your child's Sunday school
teacher? Or make an appointment to visit for a
few minutes after class to talk about your child's
spiritual development? Or have this saint over
for dinner with your family? You want to be as
much or more interested in the spiritual side of
your child's life as the academic side, don't you?
So find out, How does your child act in class?
What questions is he or she asking about spiritual things? What can you do to reinforce and
complement the Bible curriculum at home? And
most important, how can you assist the teacher
in leading your little one to a knowledge of
Jesus?

4. Double your pleasure.

Make the most of your time at church. God has given you a tremendous resource in your church, so be sure to take advantage of it. Most churches have both a worship service and a Sunday school program for both adults and children. Stay for both teaching times. If your child is old enough, sit together in church. Then during the next hour, split up as a family and go to your personal classes. Church has so much to offer you and your children. Go the extra mile and make the little choice to participate in extra times of worship, teaching, and fellowship. For a fraction of your total week, you get so much! What's an extra hour compared to the multiple benefits and blessings of going to church? That's not much out of the total week, but it means a lot when viewed from an eternal perspective.

5. Talk about church.

What you talk about in front of your children will give them a good indication of what's on your heart and mind. If church is important (and it is, right?), then talk about it all week. "Hey, kids, it's only three more days 'til youth night, Awana, Bible study. Let's go over your verses and look at your lesson." Take every opportunity to make going to church something your kids look forward to. "You're going to see your good friend Tommy...or Suzie...or hear your youth leader teach." If you do your part, what's important to you will be important to your children. So talk it up! Open your heart and lips and bless your kids of all ages by talking about church.

6. Read "Generations of Excuses."

I've added this insightful and clever article on the pages that follow. With your favorite cup of tea or soda, relax and read it for yourself. Look at the "little choices" made along the way—subtle little choices—and the effects that lasted for generations to come. Pause, pray, and see if your family might be making any of these same little choices. And then...well, you know what to do. Take your family to church!

Generations of Excuses[8]
by Mary Louise Kitsen

Dear Joan,

What a beautiful baby boy Ben and I have been blessed with! I cannot begin to tell you the joy he has brought to us.

You asked how Mrs. Miller is doing in church since her accident. They tell me she manages her wheelchair with amazing ease. She's still teaching Sunday school too. To tell you the truth, Ben and I haven't been to church since Timmy was born. It's just so difficult with a new baby. And I worry that he'll catch something. So many people have colds right now. When Timmy is just a little bigger, it will be so much easier.

Love, Sarah

Dear Joan,

Can you believe our Timmy is a year old already? He's so healthy and active—just beautiful.

No, we haven't really started attending church regularly yet. Timmy cried so hard when I tried to leave him in the nursery that I just could not do it. But he was just too noisy and active in church with us so we finally left early. The pastor came to visit. He assured us Timmy would be fine once we left him at the nursery, but I'm just not ready to force it yet. When he's just a little bigger, it will be so much easier.

Love, Sarah

Dear Joan,

However do you cope with three lively children? Timmy is into everything, and I simply cannot control him.

We still aren't attending church regularly. I tried leaving Timmy in the nursery a few Sundays back, but he didn't get along with the other children. The next week we took him into church with us, but he was all over the church. He'd be out of our pew before I could stop him. Several of the members sitting nearby were annoyed, but after all, Timmy's only three. It will be easier when he's just a little bigger.

Love, Sarah

Dear Joan,

I must be a perfectly dreadful mother! But Ben and I cannot keep our little boy under control. Last week he slipped out of our booth at a restaurant and caused a waitress to drop an entire tray of food. And last Sunday he slid out of our pew at church, and before I knew what was happening, guess where he was—right up front with the pastor! I could have fainted from embarrassment.

The pastor thinks a few hours at a preschool would be good for Timmy, but he's just four. He'll quiet down when he gets a little older.

Love, Sarah

Dear Joan,

It seems so funny to see our little boy walking off to school each morning. I thought starting him in school would be an ordeal, but Mrs. Foster must have a way with children. He seems happy as a lark.

No, Joan, we haven't started Timmy in Sunday school yet. It's just that his sister is still a new baby. And you know how hard it is getting ready to go to church with a new baby. When Sally is just a little older, it will be easier.

Love, Sarah

Dear Joan,

How the years fly by. Tim is in the fifth grade now, and little Sally just started kindergarten.

No, I'm afraid we aren't as faithful about attending Sunday school and church as we should be. With work for Ben and the children in school, we just don't get a chance to be together much during the week. And on Saturday there are always so many errands to run. Sunday is really the best time to spend some time together, and we like to start early. Last Sunday we drove to Lake Manaware. It's quite a distance. You really cannot wait until after church. These years are so special.

Love, Sarah

Dear Joan,

Teenagers certainly have a mind of their own! I simply cannot get Tim to attend Sunday school and church at all. He doesn't even want to go to youth fellowship. He thinks their activities are "dumb." He isn't getting along as well in school as Ben and I would like either. He doesn't seem to get along with his teachers or the other students. I wish we lived in a different town. There just seems to be something missing in this one.

Sally? She goes to Sunday school sometimes, but you know how little ones are. She thinks everything her brother does or thinks is perfect. But after all, the teen years are so difficult. It's a time of adjustment. When Tim matures a little more, he'll see things differently, and then his adoring little sister will too.

Love, Sarah

Dear Joan,

How I wish you and Tom could have made the wedding. It was so very beautiful. Tim looked so handsome, and his bride was just a vision. The church was filled, and everything was so lovely.

No, Tim and his bride haven't started attending church regularly yet. But after all, they are newlyweds. They enjoy just being together. So young and so in love. But they'll settle down in a little while, and then church will become a part of their lives.

Love, Sarah

Dear Joan,

Ben and I are grandparents! Tim and his Margie have the most darling baby boy you could ever hope to see. We are all so proud of him.

Church? Well, Ben and I just don't seem to go as often as we should. Ben's been promoted at the office again, and he sometimes plays golf with his boss on Sunday morning. And Sally is a teen now, and she's got her own interests. When things change, we'll get to church more often.

Tim and Margie? Oh, they can't really manage church right now. You know how hard it is with a new baby. And I warned Margie about letting the baby get exposed to colds that seem to be going around right now. When the baby is a little bigger, it will be easier. I'm sure they'll become active in church. After all, Tim was raised in a Christian home by Christian parents....He has a good example to follow....

Love, Sarah

8

*T*each Your Children to Pray

One of His disciples said to Him,
"Lord, teach us to pray."

LUKE 11:1

hildren seem to naturally desire to pray. Very few little ones will not gladly bow their heads to pray "grace" or say bedtime prayers. They want to pray! Even the baby in a highchair loves the ritual—fold hands into a fist, scrunch eyes shut, press head on folded fingers, take a peek or two, and spout out something resembling "Amen!" when the prayer is finished.

In times of fear or bewilderment, children sense the need to pray too. Again, they want to pray. I well remember an elementary schoolteacher in the Los Angeles public school system telling me that on the first day school reopened after the killer 6.8 Northridge earth-quake, her little students gathered around her. They clung to her as large aftershocks continued to roll through the area. One or two of the children even asked her if she could please pray for them, pray with them.

Because it was unlawful for my friend to pray with her students, she did what she *could* do. She gathered the children together and let them bow their heads and close their eyes for a moment of silence so they could pray as they knew how during that time.

I'm sure you scraped a knee (or two!) as a child, or took a bad fall (or two!). And you probably did what I did and turned to a parent. Somehow mom or dad made things all right, and you felt better right away. And if you were really fortunate, that parent also prayed with you.

In our family, our two little girls, with all the normal wear-and-tear of falls, scrapes, and bruises, came to either Jim or me. And we listened. We cared. We kissed boo-boos. We doctored cuts and wounds. We went to the emergency room for stitches. And we prayed. As time went by, the "falls, scrapes, and bruises" came more under the interpersonal relationship category and the resultant hurt feelings, broken friendships, break-ups, and losses.

And still today when our grown daughters have very good news to share or suffer a devastating disappoint-ment, we get a phone call. And then, once again, we listen, we rejoice or weep, we care, we seek to mend or help or comfort—whatever is needed. And we always pray, right on the phone.

Dear mom, prayer is important to our children at all ages and stages. And we bless and better their lives when we let them see and hear us pray—when we pray for them, when we pray with them...and especially when we teach them to pray. It's one more way we love them. And it's one more way we train them up for life, especially for the future when we won't always be available and they're on their own. And, blessing upon blessing, it's one more way we train them to serve God as they enter into the personal privilege and ministry of prayer.

The Optimum Mom

We've already met the optimum mom in this vital area of being a praying mom and a mom who teaches her children to pray. Her name was Hannah, and Samuel was her little guy. Hannah poured out a magnificent, powerful worship prayer to God when she left little Samuel at the temple in Shiloh (1 Samuel 2:1-10). And it's probable that, kneeling beside her, was three-year-old Samuel.

It's no wonder that the little boy Samuel—who more than likely eavesdropped on that mighty prayer from his mom's heart after God—grew up to be a great man and a man of great and mighty prayer himself. We first see the boy Samuel praying

> *May each of us be saved from the sin of prayerlessness!*[1]

and talking with God in the sanctuary as a youth (1 Samuel 3:3-20). Commenting on this scene, Matthew Henry writes regarding Samuel: "He worshipped the Lord there, that is he said his prayers. His mother, designing him for the sanctuary, took particular care to train him up to that which was to be his work in the sanctuary."[2]

Later we witness the boy-become-man-become-prophet-and-priest praying...

> ...for the nation in a time of grave trouble (1 Samuel 7:9).
>
> ...for a king for God's people (1 Samuel 8:6).
>
> ...for God to justify his displeasure with the people over their desire for a king (1 Samuel 12:17-18).
>
> ...with a grieving heart due to King Saul's disobedience (1 Samuel 15:11).
>
> ...for discernment of God's will in anointing a new king, David (1 Samuel 16:1-12).

Where, we wonder, did he learn to pray so faithfully and fervently? Probably at Momma Hannah's knee!

Other Praying Moms

One of my red-letter days as a mom was the day I first read this appeal to moms:

> The heathen mother takes her babe to the idol temple, and teaches it to clasp its little hands before its forehead, in the attitude of prayer, long before it can utter a word. As soon as it can walk, it is taught to gather a few flowers or fruits, or put a little rice upon

a banana-leaf, and lay them upon the altar before the idol god. As soon as it can utter the names of its parents, so soon it is taught to offer up its petitions before the images. Who ever saw a heathen child that could speak, and not pray? Christian mothers, why is it that so many children grow up in this enlightened land without learning to pray?[3]

I admit, I was letting my little ones grow up without learning to pray. I was allowing the days, years, and opportunities to slide by without teaching my girls to pray. This example hit me so hard as a mom of little people that I saved it. And frankly, it was just the fuel I needed to get the flame of prayer going in their hearts.

Other moms helped to show me how to teach my children to pray. (And, you guessed it, I also saved these inspiring words as I read them.)

Valerie Elliot Shepard (a mom herself to eight children) wrote this of her famous mom, Elisabeth Elliot: "Every night when she put me to bed, she sang and prayed for the two of us."[4]

Billy Graham's biography reports that "Billy's mother encouraged him to take part—beginning with a sentence prayer rehearsed in advance—in the family's daily devotions and to memorize scripture verses."[5]

No matter what they say or how they act, kids of all ages want to know about prayer. In fact, as we noted earlier, 91 percent of 13-year-olds pray to God during a typical week.[6] One teen, when asked what he wished his parents had done differently, said, "We should have had a family devotion time on a consistent basis, or at least prayed together each night." Still another added, "Step-by-step help in methods of Bible study and prayer would have better equipped me for life on my own."

Teens generally live lonely lives, despite the gang that's always around. So be sure to impress on your teens that God is interested in them and in whatever bothers or stretches them. When they enter new phases or must decide about their activities, encourage them to pray.[7]

> *You cannot lift your children to a higher level than that on which you live yourself.*

Yes, you'll pray with them. But point them toward personal prayer. Give them the gift of a super-special journal that reflects their personality and interests, a pen you know they'll like, and show them how to make and keep a prayer list. Help them to also create a schedule that contains a 5- or 10-minute slot for prayer. And above all else, let them see and hear you pray. Your example and your dedication is a priceless teacher.

Moms ask me all the time how Jim and I handled teen quiet times in our household. One thing we did was have everyone get up—and wake up! Then we had a set time of 30 minutes for each person in the house to be alone for "devotions." It was the household "quiet time." Doors were shut, and all was still.

And no, we didn't know what our teens were doing behind the doors. And no, we didn't surprise them or knock on their doors to check up on them. But we did provide the instruction, structure, books, tools, and time for spiritual growth to take place—spiritual growth that included praying about the issues of their lives.

A Walk Through Your Day

When you get a minute to yourself (and I'm smiling as I say that!), walk through your normal (there goes another smile!) day. Think of what you and your children have to give thanks for and where you need God's help. Then show them the way. Is it...

> ...breakfast time? Thank God for food and pray for a good day.

> ...devotional time? Verbalize to God what's been learned and ask for His help in applying it.

> ...work or chore time? Ask for God's help with character development, for your kids to do their work heartily to the Lord—not just for mom (Colossians 3:23)!

> ...leaving for school time? Share in a brief group prayer and a group hug in the doorway.

...homeschool lesson time? Pray for God to help you to teach clearly and your child to learn, for both of you to do a good job.

...homework time? Teach your children to ask God for help with any and all projects.

...arriving home from school time? Praise God for another day of education and a safe return to home-sweet-home.

...snack time? Give thanks for food (again!) and pray about what's happening next, what each one of you is preparing to do next.

...go to work time? Send your older kids off to jobs with a prayer and a kiss. They'll need it! Things are tough out in the world.

...another meal time? At any and all meals be faithful that "foods which God created [are] received with thanksgiving" (1 Timothy 4:3).

...bedtime? Pray something like the sentiment of Susanna Wesley's end-of-day prayer: "I give Thee praise, O God, for 'a well-spent day.'"[8] (And P.S.: Don't just pray with your children. Send them to sleep with a kiss!)

As a mom I aim for the apostle Paul's attitude. He told those he prayed for, "I have you in my heart" (Philippians 1:7). And because I carry my children in my heart (just like you do), I find myself praying always...and fervently...for them.

Prompting Prayer

As you teach your children to pray, prompts from you help. Be creative and proactive. Ask them questions. Not only will you be prompting them to pray, but you'll get a glimpse into what's going on in their lives. Begin small. For really little ones, begin with a muttered or hearty "Amen!" Then move to sentence prayers during grace at meal times. Teach them to answer your prompts,

> *Pray that your children will "continue in the things which [they] have learned... knowing from whom [they] have learned them."*
>
> 2 TIMOTHY 3:14

"Jesus, thank You for..."

"Jesus, please help me to..."

"Jesus, please help _____ to..."

Have them pray sentence prayers for any big or small blessing in their little lives. Then advance the level of depth as their ages advance.

Ask, "What would you like to thank Jesus for tonight? Today? Right now? Let's not forget to say 'thank You' to

Jesus!" No matter the age, from toddlers on up, they can answer this question...and pray about it.

Ask, "What are you worried about? Sad about? Let's tell God about it right now. He can take care of it." And away you go, sharing in the scary issues in their little—and big—lives...and helping them learn to cast their cares upon the Lord (1 Peter 5:7).

Ask, "What is your biggest challenge today? What would you like to ask God to help you with? Let's ask Him now." Older kids have school pressures (tests, grades, performance), peer pressure (friends—both boy- and girlfriends!), job pressures, and pressure to stand up for what's right and speak up for their faith in Christ.

Ask, "Can you think of a special friend we can pray for? How can we ask God to help him or her?" This prompt pushes children to think beyond themselves, to begin to take notice of others and their needs, to be concerned for others. As they add praying for others to their daily prayers, their character grows.

Ask, "What do you think your dad/brother/sister needs help with? What kindnesses can you do for them to make their lives easier? Let's ask God to help us all." It's never too early to work on family love.

Praying Always...for All Things

The New Testament writers summed up the importance of prayer best for us: We should...

> pray always with all kinds of prayers and requests (Ephesians 6:18),
>
> pray without ceasing (1 Thessalonians 5:17),

pray one for another (James 5:16),

pray about everything (Philippians 4:6),

pray fervently (James 5:16), and

pray continually (Acts 6:4).

The goal is to teach our children to do the same as we strive to fulfill these instructions ourselves.

As you and your family deal with the everyday cares of life, make it a point to pray. As my former pastor loved to say, "Prayer is spiritual breathing. Every breath in should result in a prayer out." That, mom, is your goal with your children. Let them see that prayer is a natural, first response to everything. Here are two more scenarios that merit your spontaneous prayers, your "spiritual breathing."

Pray with their friends. When your kids have friends, neighbors, or schoolmates over, no matter what their ages, pray grace with them at the table or with a snack. If your kids have guests sleeping over, pray over everyone when you "tuck them in." If their friends share a problem or a worry in the midst of a conversation, pray with them...just like you would your own. You see, you're a praying mom! You can't do otherwise!

Pray on the phone. When our family arrived home from the mission field, our girls were junior high age. As "missionary kids"—MKs—back in America, they suddenly seemed like they were from another era of time. They were out of it, behind the times culturally. When they entered junior high, surprisingly, they began to call home during the day, usually during lunch. At first I couldn't figure it out, but at last I got it. They had no friends, no one to eat with or talk to. So if they "had to make a phone call," their loneliness, confusion, and awkwardness didn't stand out. So I began praying with them on the phone...for a good rest of the day...and telling them I'd see them in just a few hours.

Jim too prayed with our daughters on the phone. Even to this day, when they call he always says something like, "Let's thank God." Or "Let's pray about this." Or "I don't want to hang up until we pray."

Even though it may not be verbalized or requested outright, kids phone home for assurance, to touch base, to talk to someone who loves them and cares about the details of their lives, for something familiar, for love, for wisdom. When you and I don't pray with them...why, they could have called anyone in the world and gotten advice! They could have dialed 911 to *talk* to someone, but they dialed you so you could *pray* with them. You can give them something no one else can—your prayers.

Here's a principle I've tried to live by that was passed on to me from an older mentor. She said, "Elizabeth, remember that everything you do and don't do teaches." So, dear mom, when you pray, you teach your children to pray. When you pray with your kids, you teach them to pray. When you pray with them on the phone...in the car...at the door...when they eat...when they get home...when they go to bed...with their friends, you teach them to pray.

And when you don't pray with them, you are teaching them that prayer isn't that important. So speak up. Open your mouth and pray...and pray...and pray. Don't give your prized children even the slightest opportunity to think you are not a praying mom. You are...and they must know it. Let them see—and hear—your passion for God, for praying to God, for them, and for praying for them. As a mom after God's own heart—a mom who prays—you will teach them much about prayer.

From a Dad's Heart

Some years ago I attended a pastor's conference and was again challenged with the importance of teaching my children to pray. One of the speakers gave a testimonial of how his father had spent quality time with him and his two sisters every night as they were growing up. The man's father wasn't a pastor or seminary theologian. He was just a layman in his church, an ordinary guy who would gather his children around him every bedtime and read a small portion of Bible to them. He would ask each child what the passage meant, and he would give his thoughts on the passage. Finally, the father would have each child pray about the happenings of his (or her) day and anything he was to face the next day. The godly father would finalize the bedtime ritual with an all-encompassing prayer.

The speaker went on to say that this nightly routine lasted for as long as any of the children were living at home, some into their twenties. Needless to say, it wasn't surprising to hear that, by God's grace, all three children grew up to be strong, vibrant Christians.

I want to encourage you to do two things. First, be sure you are praying with your children.

You don't have control over your husband,
over whether he is a Christian or not and over
his desire to be involved with parental and
spiritual input. But you do have control over
your time and priorities. Like my mom did with
me, while dad is in the living room watching
TV, tuck your little and big ones into bed and
pray with and for them. It only takes a few
minutes. Like the parent above who made a
dynamic impression on his son and two daughters, do whatever it takes to spend quality time
with your kids.

Then, with much prayer, if your husband is
a believer, move toward helping him understand the importance of his involvement with
teaching the children to pray. He may already
be doing this—and that's ideal! Don't fail to
give him a regular pat on the back for his participation. However, if he is not as involved as
he should be or could be, share with him what
you are learning, and ask for his help in this
most important child-raising activity.

The father I mentioned wasn't a dynamic
preacher or church leader. He was just a man—
a dad—who loved his children, loved God, and
wanted his children to love God too. So pray
that together you and your man will consider
"teaching your children to pray" one of your
highest and most sacred duties as Christian parents.

Little Choices That Reap Big Blessings

1. Memorize "The Lord's Prayer."

Are you wondering where to begin? Begin where Jesus began with His disciples, His children (so to speak). Jesus' disciples repeatedly saw and heard Him praying. Finally they asked, "Lord, teach us to pray" (Luke 11:1). And Jesus answered them by showing them exactly how, even providing the words for them. He said, "When you pray, say" and then He gave them what we call The Lord's Prayer (Matthew 6:9-13).

If that prayer is what Jesus' own family of disciples needed, then it's a good thing for your children too. Make a group project of memorizing and praying this prayer with your children. Pray it occasionally at mealtime, at bedtime, and on special occasions to keep it fresh in everyone's heart and mind.

2. Pray as a lifestyle.

The Bible says "pray without ceasing" (1 Thessalonians 5:16). Make this command your personal prayer motto, not only because this is to be your attitude as a Christian, but also because of the model you provide for your children.

To follow-through on this constant attitude of prayer, pray all day long with an eye on the clock. Where are your children? What classes are they in? Are they taking their test, giving their speech? Is it lunchtime? Recess? Are they on the school bus? At practice? In a study group? At work? At youth group or Bible study? Driving the car? Be known to your children as a praying mom.

3. Share sentence prayers at the dinner table.

If it's okay with your husband, and he doesn't feel awkward about it, have him ask everyone to go around the table and in one sentence thank God for something that happened in their lives that day. (And here's a hint: It helps if you've prepared everyone to be on the lookout during the day for what they want to especially thank God for in the evening.) If you do this on a routine basis, your children will begin to automatically notice and think all day about what God is doing in their lives. They too will become trained to "in everything give thanks" (1 Thessalonians 5:18).

4. Read from a book of prayers.

There are many books of "Common Prayers," or books of the prayers of great men and women of the past. The Puritans were famous for their books of prayers, *The Valley of Vision* being one of them.[9] If he's up for it, have dad read one prayer each morning and then ask each person to pray a sentence prayer reflecting the theme of the written prayer. That's all he has to do! If dad would rather not be a part of the prayer, then do this exercise privately with your children when dad is gone or busy.

5. Create a family prayer list.

What better way can you think of for teaching your children the importance of prayer and how to pray than by showing them the answers to their very own prayers! How is this done? By creating a family prayer list. Each day as you discuss the activities of the day and the needs of others, you, or one of the older kids, become "recording secretary" and create a list as you ask, "What would you like to ask God to help you with? Can you think of a special friend we can pray for? I heard about someone at church who needs our prayers. How can we ask God to help him or her?"

Again, prompts like these cause kids to think beyond themselves, to care about others and their hurts and needs. As your family prays for others, personal and spiritual growth occurs. Then at the end of the day, at dinner or at bedtime, or the next morning, follow-up on the prayers. Ask, "How has God answered your prayers about...?" Then write the answer next to the prayer request. Save the answers and review God's goodness often with the children. Show them how He is working in their lives through prayer.

6. Pray daily with each child at bedtime.

Whether it's you or your husband or both, relish the nightly ritual. Even plan for it—what you want to say to each child, any verses you want to share, what you want to pray over each child. In the years to come, your children will look back and say how much they appreciated these times. And they'll do the same for their little ones. Again, your kids may protest at first, but go ahead. They'll go to sleep and then wake up the next day knowing *someone* is concerned for them...and that God is watching over them.

Bedtime prayers will also become a time when your children often open up and share their heart concerns, fears, and joys with you. Why? Because they know you'll pray about it right there on the spot. And the blessing is often reversed: One teen shared, "My mother would kneel beside my bed at night and pray for me before telling me good night. It was often during the prayers that she was able to communicate her feelings or concerns to me."[10] Don't miss out on these priceless times.

9

Try Your Best

*And whatever you do, do it heartily,
as to the Lord and not to men.*

COLOSSIANS 3:23

love the verses in the Bible that point to God's grace. Maybe that's because I need so much of it! Especially in the Mom Department. I'm guessing that's true of every mom because of the delicate nature of child-raising. We love God. We love our children. We want to follow God's instructions for us as moms. And we want to do our best. We really do!

But here's how it goes for me. I have so many passionate desires, dreams, and prayers for myself as a mom and for my children. So I move forward, full-steam ahead. I do everything I think I'm supposed to do—and more!—for a while. And then there's a bad day. I slip up or parenting seems more demanding or less rewarding than it was yesterday. Somehow something got accelerated or something went wacky. Something changed and, amazingly, what worked yesterday didn't work today.

And then I'm right back down on my knees. Again I'm lifting up my prayers and cries to God for wisdom, for discernment, for His love-joy-peace-patience-self-control, for His strength...and, most of all, for His grace.

And I start all over again. After my flop or lapse or wake-up call, God points me once again to square one, to my priorities as a woman and my purpose as a mom.

Dear fellow mom, these are the facts of life for any and every mother. Being a mother is a commitment, a responsibility, and a calling from God...for a lifetime. And being a mom is our highest joy *and* our greatest challenge. So what can we do? Every time I ask myself this question, the answer is always the same—we can only try to do our best. It's one more way we love our children.

As we head into this subject in this most important chapter, let me share six attitudes and approaches that will help you do your best. And notice I said "attitudes and approaches." These will not be things to *do*. No, they will be more like things to *think* as you approach your "Mommyhood"[2] each new day.

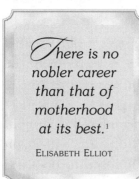

There is no nobler career than that of motherhood at its best.[1]

ELISABETH ELLIOT

1. Know Who You Are

A red-letter day in my life arrived on a Sunday afternoon.

That's the day Jim and I sat down to write out some life-time goals. Our hearts were searching for direction for our service to Christ, for our marriage, and for our family and us as parents. Our girls were young—still in diapers. Jim and I eagerly wanted to do the right thing, so my husband prayed...and away we went, off with the Lord for a few hours of brainstorming and goal-setting while our little ones napped.

Well, at the end of the afternoon, I emerged with three life goals in mind—goals that would definitely have to be accomplished by the energizing power of the Holy Spirit if they were to happen at all. And there was no doubt as I looked at them that they would demand some tremendous personal growth—like a 180-degree turn-around!

My Number One goal that came out of that afternoon of prayer and heart-searching was stated this way: "To be supportive and encouraging to my husband and chil-dren." These are simple words. There's nothing earth-shattering here (unless you had been living for yourself and neglecting your family...like I had!). But since that memorable day, I have known exactly who I am and what it is I'm supposed to do—I am a wife and a mother. I am to love my husband and love my children. In short, on that sunny Sunday, my life became, for the first time, focused.

And today, as I'm sitting here thinking about where I was...and where I wanted to go...and thinking about you...and where you might be...and where you might want to go, I realize that any lifetime goal is just that—a goal that will require a lifetime to accomplish. But this one goal forced me to answer a most significant question: "Who am I?"

I believe with all my heart that your best—or my best...or anyone's best—is born out of knowing who you are. So I'll ask: Do you know who you are? If you have children, you are one of God's moms. That's who you are.

2. Know What It Is You Do

I addressed what it means to love God first and foremost in *Loving God with All Your Mind.*[3] Loving God with all your heart, soul, and mind is—and always will be—our ultimate priority (Matthew 22:37). And being a loving

The young women [are]...to love their children.

Titus 2:4

wife is covered in other books I've written.[4] But my role as a mom is what this book is all about. My goal to focus on my family forced me to realize that, based on Titus 2:3-5, next to loving God and loving my husband, loving my children was my highest human priority and responsibility.

Oh, what freedom! To finally know who I am *and* what it is I am to do! From that point on, I began to focus my efforts and energies into being the best mom I knew how to be. And you know, with this focus life got a lot easier. Before knowing who I was and what I was to do, I was trying to be all things to all people—including myself—and I was failing miserably. I realized I couldn't serve all those people and interests at the same time. I couldn't please everyone and do everything. I was going to have to make choices about who I needed to serve.

So I chose to focus on my family. And that choice also meant I needed to focus on myself and growing in Christ—so I did just that. I focused on growing in God's grace and in my knowledge of Him through His Word and in my walk with Him. And I soon grew to better understand the amazing assignment God had given me— that of being a mom—a mom after His very own heart! I began (like you are right now) to read books about Christian parenting, about training my little ones, about teaching them godly wisdom and character.

It's now been 30 years since that bright goal-setting day. And I have to say, the goals I laid out that afternoon have never budged, changed, shifted, or evolved. Yes, my nest is empty as I'm sitting here pouring out my heart to you, but I'm still a mom to this day. That will *never* change. And glory-upon-glories, I'm a grandmom to seven little ones too.

And I have to be honest, if I really want to move into fear-mode, all I have to do is start wondering, "What if…I hadn't set those goals? What if…I hadn't gotten things straight with God? What if…I hadn't made some hard and important decisions? What if…things had continued to drift along…in the wrong direction?"

All of this to say, I want to encourage you to take your own hour or two (yes, I'm smiling!) and think through who you are and what it is you do—or what you are supposed to do. Putting your answers on paper will simplify your life, clarify your purpose, and revolutionize your life as a mother. It will provide the focus that is required for trying to do your best as a mom. It will provide you with 30, 40, 50 years (only God knows how many actual years) of knowing, every single day, exactly who you are and what it is you are to do.

Dear one, realize too that on every single one of your days, the world will be sending you signals that you are a nobody unless you are a focused, sold-out working woman. The world says being a mom is old-fashioned. That you need to take care of yourself. That you're supposed to be Number One. That your kids will make it just fine without your constant care. But the world is wrong! You can rest in your heart and know with all of the confidence and strength in the world who you are and what it is you are to do.

3. Realize You Cannot Serve Two Masters

I now understand that I was learning the value of the principle Jesus laid down for us that applies equally to all areas of life: We cannot serve two masters equally. Jesus stated, "No one can serve two masters; for either he will hate the one and love the other, or else he will be loyal to the one and despise the other" (Matthew 6:24). Although Jesus was speaking of loving God or loving money, His remarks regarding divided loyalties apply to many areas in a woman's life—even that of being a mom.

Here's how this principle worked in my life. I had two little girls, ages one and two...but I also had a desire for an advanced education degree. So I enrolled in college with a full load of classwork, found a babysitter, began dropping my babies off at daycare before daylight, and picking them up after dark. I was definitely serving one master (going to school) over another (being a mom).

Then, when I became a Christian and wrote down my goals, I realized that to serve my new and forever Master, Jesus, meant I also needed to serve my husband and children. So I dropped the master's program and began the real "Master's Program"! You might say I began earning a Master's degree in Mothering.

Please, don't get me wrong. I'm not saying you can't or shouldn't have a job or a career or be enrolled in school. We moms are the absolute best when it comes to managing, juggling, and balancing life's demands. We are the world's finest. That's something else we do! But what I am saying is that if you find yourself (like I did) viewing your job or career, schooling or hobbies, even your ministry, as your master, as the focus of your life, time, and energy, then you've drifted over a line that will make it next to impossible to give your best to your children.

Divided loyalties lead to diluted living.

Oh, there'll be good times. You'll have some quality spurts with your children. But you'll find this *other* thing tugging at your heart and mind. Your energies will quickly turn elsewhere. Believe me, I know what I'm talking about, both as a mom who fell into this category for a while and as a child of a career mom.

I'm praying that, with God's help and by His grace, you will begin to understand who you are—a mom—and that what you do is give your best to your kids. Except for God and your husband, everything else is secondary.

4. Keep It Simple

I recently read some startling statistics about moms. Did you know that "70 percent of American moms say they find motherhood today 'incredibly stressful.' Thirty percent of mothers of young children reportedly suffer from depression. Nine hundred and nine women in Texas recently told researchers they find taking care of their kids about as much fun as cleaning their house, slightly less pleasurable than cooking, and a whole lot less enjoyable than watching TV."[5]

Oh, do I ever see myself here on certain days (you know, those crazy loser days every mom drowns in once in a while). All I can say is it helps to keep things simple. That's perhaps the greatest survival tactic for moms. The word "stressful" means strained. It's a condition of tension caused by too much pressure. To relieve the strain and reduce the tension and pressure, simplify things. For instance...

> ...make fewer trips out in the car. Run less personal (notice I didn't say needful) errands when the kids are with you. Choose one or two days to go out for errands each week...instead of every day.

> ...make simpler meals and serve them in a simpler manner. Eat earlier at night. Get the kids ready for bed—and in bed—earlier. End your day earlier.

...well, I could go on and mention things
like organizing and cleaning out clutter,
but for most of us that might put us over
the edge by adding even more pressure!

As you think about keeping things simple, picture the classic fable of the tortoise and the hare. Who won the race between these two? The tortoise. Why? Because the tortoise was steady, easy going, forward moving, and unpressured. The hare, however, was all over the place, running here, running there, frazzled, and unfocused. In all of the hustle and bustle, the hare lost sight of the goal. I'm sure you get the message: Keep it simple, steady as she goes, and don't lose sight of the goal—of being a mom after God's own heart.

5. Don't Go It Alone

In the Bible Mary, the mother of Jesus, had Elizabeth (Luke 1). Paul had Timothy. Elijah had Elisha. Moses had Aaron. All these mighty-for-God men—and moms!—needed the encouragement and the camaraderie of like-minded people. There will be more on this important aspect of survival for moms in the final chapter. But for now, remember that God has surrounded you with other moms. Surely in your church there are those in your same boat—the mommy boat. There are also older women who are a step or two ahead of you in the mothering game, and maybe even some who have finished the course.

God has set the church up to include younger women and moms who can and need to learn from older women and moms, and also older women and moms who can pass on their wisdom and lend support to those who are younger and less experienced. Hook up with other moms. Let them steer you in the right direction—God's direction. Allow them to provide you with wisdom—God's wisdom. Welcome any and all helping hands, praying hearts, and much-needed encouragement.

6. Take One Day at a Time

If you think about it for even a millisecond, you might begin to see mothering as an overwhelming task. Here you are, entrusted with a human soul that will live for eternity. Of course, God is ultimately responsible for the eternal destiny of that child, but humanly speaking, you and your husband are responsible for his or her physical, mental, and spiritual development. Now before you get too anxious and have a nervous breakdown, take to heart Jesus' calming advice about focusing your efforts on today only: "Don't be anxious about tomorrow. God will take care of your tomorrow too. Live one day at a time" (Matthew 6:34 TLB).

My friend and fellow mom, just focus on making today count. Try your best to be the best mother you can be...just for today. Oh, believe me, you will fail on some days, but don't give up. The reward is too great to not give it your all each and every day. Cherish your one day. Welcome it. Plan it. Live it. Enjoy it. Evaluate it. Adjust it. (I just received an email from a first-time home-school mom who admitted she was very task-oriented, but, after some evaluating, planning, and adjusting, was learning to "have fun" with the kids. She wrote, "We are having a blast!")

And what will happen when you begin to live one day at a time? You'll find yourself stringing one "best" day after another. Don't get in a hurry to have a season pass. Pass it will! Don't wish away the nursing infant at your breast and the fact that his or her care takes your time away from other activities. Don't wish away the crawler or toddler who's into everything. Don't wish away the "terrible (or is it terrific?) twos," the troublesome teen years, or hectic summers. What matters is

> *Sow your best efforts today, and reap God's abundant blessings tomorrow.*

where your heart is and enjoying the days you have with your children.

Then when you have finally fashioned, with God's help, your child into a beautiful, godly life, you can stand back with amazement and thanksgiving. What you will be looking at is a life that is ready to take his or her place in society as a strong, vibrant Christian. A life that represents God's next generation. A life that will start the process all over again in another home with other new little souls. As the psalmist declared, "[The LORD's] truth endures to all generations" (Psalm 100:5).

Heart Response

I'm sure I've said this before (and may again!), but it's worth repeating. When it comes to your mothering, it's a matter of the heart. Focus your heart firmly on giving your all to each day as it arrives, and don't worry about your entire life. All God is asking is that you give being a mom your all...just for today. It's just a 24-hour span. And even some of that span (though never enough!) will be spent sleeping (if all goes well!).

And remember, giving all your heart to practice right priorities begins with God. Therefore, seek Him first thing each new day. Acknowledge Him. Spend time with Him. Pray and present your day to Him, along with its "trouble" (Matthew 6:34)—you know, all the accidents, curve balls, interruptions, and Plan B's that will most surely arise during your day. Draw energy from Him. Sharpen your focus before God into a settled determination.

Next, lay your priorities as a wife before God. Then put your high calling of Mom before Him. Reaffirm who you are and what it is you are to do...just for today. Review your priorities—what's important to you, and most important, what's important to God. Turn every area of life over to Him...just for today.

Finally, as you walk through your day, "in all your ways acknowledge Him, and He shall direct your paths" (Proverbs 3:6). As each issue and option comes at you, stop, think, and pray—even if it's just for a split second. Ask God's advice. Ask for His wisdom (James 1:5). Involve Him in your every thought during the day, your every word spoken to your little male and female treasures. Make Him the center of all that you do. When you follow this practice, you'll discover that He is truly guiding you step-by-step through your day, assisting you as you do your best...just for today. He will lead and empower you to work to accomplish His purposes, one of those being that you are a mom.

I have a few verses that keep me going as a mom and inspire me to keep on giving my all. I use them almost as one, and I use them every day, all day long: "But one thing I do... [and] I can do all things through Christ who strengthens me" (Philippians 3:13 and 4:13). You see, the apostle Paul, who wrote these words, had a goal. And that goal required—and consumed—all his energy. He never took his eyes off the goal...nor should we. He gave his all...and so should we. And what did Paul do when things got tough, when the path turned uphill, when his energy waned? He simply drew on his riches in Christ Jesus (Philippians 4:19). Why, he could do *all* things through Christ, his power source! And so can you.

From a Dad's Heart

Before you were a mom, you were a wife. Hopefully, you do everything you can to support and love your husband (Titus 2:4). You do your best. You try to do him "good and not evil all the days of [your] life" (Proverbs 31:12). Well, keep up the good work! Your marriage will be blessed by God, and you will have a great friend in your husband long after the children are grown and gone.

But what about Proverbs 31:27: "She watches over the ways of her household"? Are you also continually "watching" as a sentinel over your home and your children? In Bible times a "watchman" had one function, one purpose—to watch and warn. You, as a mom, have an important purpose as ordained by God—love your children (Titus 2:4). How is this to be done?

Elizabeth has been helping you see how this calling fleshes out in your life. You love your children by guarding them from the evils and pitfalls they encounter outside the walls of your home. And the best way to do this is to train them in the ways of God so they are prepared when they leave the house. And this training starts early. The communists said, "Give us a child for the first six years of life and then you can have it back." Why six? They knew, along with science and educators, that the majority of foundational learning comes by age six. In six years the communists could so thoroughly indoctrinate a child in their ideology that he or she was theirs for life.

Most parents, even Christian parents, put off training until their child "gets older." By the time many Christian parents put spiritual training into full gear, humanly speaking, it's almost too late. The child is already set in the world's ways.

Christian mom, are you trying your best to love, train, watch, and warn? Or are you a little preoccupied with other things? Have you gotten side-tracked? Has your primary focus in life been diverted? Have you subtly stopped watching over your children? Have you relied on others to teach and train your children? Don't give your children over to the world. Fight for their souls! Do battle with the forces of evil. Watch and warn, pray and act. Jobs and hobbies and other activities come and go, but the soul left to the world's pull can be lost for eternity. Pray, do your best, and trust the results to God.

And what if you are having to go it alone? What if you are a single mom having to raise your children for life and for God alone? Or what if your husband travels a lot, or is deployed by the military, or works long or odd hours, or is unsupportive in child-raising efforts? Never forget that in reality, you—and every mom—are never alone. God is there! He knows your situation. He knows what every one of His moms is up against and the difficulties you encounter. He knows your children and their struggles. But He still asks one thing of you—that, as a mom, you try your best. Thank Him that His "grace is sufficient for you" and His "strength is made perfect in [your] weakness" (2 Corinthians 12:9)!

Little Choices That Reap Big Blessings

1. Evaluate your normal weekly schedule.

Mentally list your many roles and responsibilities. What little choices have you been making in terms of activities, time investments, and personal pursuits that are consuming the majority of your physical time? Your mental energies? How do these choices compare with God's choices in Titus 2:4: "The young women [are] to love their husbands, to love their children"?

2. Make a fresh start today.

As a busy mom, I'm sure you are shocked at the amount of time you can sometimes spend on pursuits other than that of being the best mom you can be. But as you evaluate your schedule, start turning things around. What little choices can you make today to say "no" to other activities in order to say "yes" to your children? The great preacher, Charles Haddon Spurgeon, put it this way: "Take care of your lambs, or where will you get your sheep from?"

3. Lavish them with love.

Write "Three Ways I Can Love My Children Today" on a 3″ x 5″ card and list three choices you can make today that say "I love you, I cherish you" to the little and big people who make up your family. Make a fresh card each morning for the next few days. God's love for you is fresh and new every morning...and your love for your loved ones can be too. Look for new and personal little ways to demonstrate your love to your children.

4. Start being a more involved mom.

If your schedule is keeping you from being more involved in your children's lives, pray, and start making the little choices that will result in a dramatic turnaround. Start by choosing to be more involved in the daily process of their lives. Choose to be a part of their daily training. It's only natural for people—and especially children of all ages—to stray and run wild when left to themselves. As the proverb puts it, "A child left to himself brings shame to his mother" (Proverbs 29:15). A mom needs to remember that children thrive in their mom's very presence when given strong, sure limits. The limits you set are an indication of your love.

7. Schedule your own goal-setting session.

Pardon my smile for putting this as a "little choice"! But really, it's a little choice to take out your calendar and choose a time to meet with God to evaluate your life. It's no problem getting to the beauty salon for a makeover that takes two hours or traveling to attend a special craft seminar to learn something new. So go for the ultimate makeover! Learn the ultimate new skills! Make the all-important little choice to reserve your own personal appointment with God. Who knows? It may just well be your own red-letter day!

Talk to God About Your Children

Be anxious for nothing,
but in everything by prayer
and supplication with thanksgiving
let your requests be made known to God.

PHILIPPIANS 4:6

I've often heard Jim teach about "the whole man." In the Greek culture of Bible times, the whole man was one who was complete in three areas of life: body, soul, and spirit. All three parts were to be trained and matured. The Greeks worked on their bodies, developed their minds, and sought a fine-tuned spiritual awareness and religious understanding. Excellence in all three areas was required in order to be considered complete or whole.

The Whole Child

This same concept applies to child-raising. We are to prepare, educate, and train "the whole child," neglecting none of these realms. Physically, we take care of our children to ensure, to the best of our ability, that they are healthy, strong, and fully developed. Mentally we make sure they are educated and trained for life. But spiritually we teach, train, show the way, *and* pray! That's because spiritual development is a battle. As the apostle Paul explained, "We do not wrestle against flesh and blood, but against principalities, against powers, against the rulers of the darkness of this age, against spiritual hosts of wickedness in the heavenly places" (Ephesians 6:12).

Who better to pray for than your children, and who better to talk to about them than God?

This is where praying and being a praying mom comes into focus. In this chapter we move to the area that accomplishes more than all of our doing for our children does. It's private. It's personal. It's done alone. And it's spiritual. I'm talking about spiritual warfare! It's nothing we do *with* our children because we do it alone, yet...somehow...it seems to accomplish amazing things *for* our children. Dear mom, it's prayer, and here are "The Top Five" items for your prayer list...the prayer list of a mom after God's own heart.

1. Pray for Your Child's Salvation

This week, while Jim and I were at a speaking event, our little grandson Ryan entered this world...four weeks early! Although we had arranged our schedule to cover his mom and family for two weeks before and after his due date, he chose to surprise us. I'm so thankful to the event coordinator who was able to print off a picture of this new little grandson for Jim and me so we could see what he looked like. Well, from that point on I found myself kissing his picture and saying, "There's the little one whose salvation I've been praying for!"

That's the way it is with our children. As my own children were growing up, I prayed daily for my two girls to become Christians, to believe in Jesus Christ as their Savior. I also prayed daily for 20-plus years for their future mates, that they would love and belong to Christ as well. And, by God's grace, our daughters and their husbands have become two Christian families with seven children. And, you guessed it, we are now in the throes of praying for God's gracious salvation of the next generation...and their spouses...and... Well, you get the picture. It's one that extends into eternity!

Dear mom, I don't know how many minutes a day you have or can set aside for prayer for your children and the salvation of their souls, but we can never underestimate its value and importance. The way I made praying for my girls through the decades happen was by creating a special tab in my prayer notebook. The tab didn't say "Children." No, it said "Katherine & Courtney." Using their names was much more

Who better to pray for a child's second birth than the mom who gave birth to that child?

personal. You see, they were (and are) a passion of mine, and my prayer time for them was (and is) an eternal investment. They were and are vitally important to me. Within that section in my notebook I had three pages that I wrote on daily:

> Page 1—General prayer requests for both.
>
> Page 2—Specific prayer requests for Katherine.
>
> Page 3—Specific prayer requests for Courtney.

With this setup I could pray for general issues for both girls—salvation, spiritual growth, safety at school, friends, godly character qualities, involvement at church. These kinds of prayers rarely change and apply to all our children, both yours and mine.

After covering the "biggies"—with eternal life being the Number One biggie—I then moved to the individual pages and prayed specifically for the concerns of each of my girls—respect for Jim and me as their parents, medical problems, habits, attitudes, any difficulties at school, problem relationships, a job interview, acceptance of their applications for college. As individual as each of your children is, that is how unique you can tailor your list for each one of them.

There are many things we moms can pray about for our children, but there's absolutely no doubt that their salvation is tops on the list. Pray what I call "The Lydia Prayer" from Acts 16:14:

Lord, please open [your child's name] heart
to accept the message of the gospel.

If and when, by God's grace, this becomes a miracu-
lous reality, then you move right on to praying for their
"sanctification"—to praying for their spiritual growth, for
their Christlikeness.

2. Pray for Your Child's Friends

Beyond the preaching and teaching that must accom-
pany and prepare the way for this key area in every
child's life—their friends—prayer is the order of every
day! Constant prayer for years and years and years! That's
because friends are such a vital area in a child's life. As
Paul stated, "Do not be deceived: 'Evil company corrupts
good habits'" (1 Corinthians 15:33). Proverbs, too,
teaches, "Make no friendship with an angry man, and
with a furious man do not go, lest you learn his ways
and set a snare for your soul" (Proverbs 22:24-25). And
so we moms pray!

Here's how praying about friends went for me as a
mom. As I listened to my daughters talk about their
friends and as I met them one by one, I put their friends'
names on my prayer list for each daughter. I prayed for
their friends' salvation and Christian character. I prayed
for their situations at home. I prayed that they be a good
influence on my girls...and my girls on them!

Also, whenever my girls were invited to a friend's
house or to do something with a friend, I prayed for
wisdom. Was it the right person? The right kind of
activity? The right amount of time (or too much)? The

right timing in their lives? (For instance, when should sleepovers and trips to the mall begin?) The right time of day? Of course I talked everything over with Jim, but I also talked everything over with my Heavenly Husband.

And friends of the opposite sex? All of the praying mentioned above goes double—and triple!—for this delicate area that calls for utmost carefulness on a mom's part. One thing that helped us tremendously was my husband's foresight. He had both of our daughters write out in their own words the Bible's standards for the kind of boyfriends they should have. These lists were written before adolescence and hormones and peer pressure set in, and they were carefully filed away. Then, when some guy came along, Jim would say, "Let's get your list, honey, and see what the standards are that you set for a boyfriend." And out came the list from the file cabinet,

Anyone who pushes you nearer to God is your friend.

and together we would all go over it. Did the young man measure up to God's profile? As the girls answered that question, decisions became obvious... regardless of emotions.

Those handwritten lists, my friend, became the guidelines we *and* our children prayed over...and over. And then, of course, if some boy did qualify, his name went right on top of Momma's Prayer List—and I mean with capital letters! Now here was *ultra*-serious business I needed to tend to with God!

If I had my way, I would ask you to *please* read daily from Proverbs with your child. Why Proverbs? First, because the dual purpose of the book of Proverbs is "to produce the skill of godly living by wisdom and instruction...and to develop discernment."[1] As the writer of Proverbs explains, the purpose of the book is "to give prudence to the simple, to the young man knowledge and discretion" (Proverbs 1:4). What a blessing for our kids! And second, because so much of this little book of wisdom has to do with different types of people and situations and how to recognize them. In everyday language, Proverbs describes those who are good and evil, righteous and unrighteous, wise and foolish. With any exposure to Proverbs, your children will have God's wisdom concerning the kinds of friends to choose to be with and those they should avoid at all costs.

But don't leave it all up to Proverbs. Pray like only a mom can! Pray the contents of Psalm 1:1-2:

> Lord, grant that [your child's name] would walk not in the counsel of the ungodly, nor stand in the path of sinners, nor sit in the seat of the scornful, but that his (or her) delight will be in the law of the Lord.

3. Pray for Your Child's Purity

I shared 1 Thessalonians 4 earlier. It's a wonderful purity verse for you to preach and teach...and pray for your kids: "For this is the will of God, your sanctification: that you should abstain from sexual immorality; that each of you should know how to possess his own vessel in sanctification and honor, not in passion of lust, like the Gentiles who do not know God; that no one should take advantage of and defraud his brother in this matter....For God did not call us to uncleanness, but in holiness" (verses 3-7). Briefly, based on these verses, you can teach, preach, and pray as follows:

- ♡ God has revealed His will concerning sexual purity.

- ♡ Steer clear of all sexual sin.

- ♡ It is possible to control your body.

- ♡ God's standards are the opposite of the world's.

- ♡ Sexual expression is reserved for marriage.

- ♡ Never tempt, tease, or take advantage of anyone sexually.

- ♡ We are called to holiness, and God will help us fulfill this calling.

Fellow praying mom, this is why we pray first for salvation for each child, and then for their friendships. Both prayer processes pave the way for this one. Turn these verses from 1 Thessalonians 4:3-7 and their instruction into a prayer that goes something like this:

> Lord, I pray that [your child's name] will keep himself (herself) from all sexual sin, that he (she) will learn how to master his (her) own body in holiness and purity, that

he (she) will not succumb to temptation or take advantage of another person, that he (she) will understand that God has called us to dedicate ourselves to holiness and the most thorough purity.

4. Pray for Your Child's Schoolwork

Are your children young? Then you as a mom get to make learning fun. But to do this requires time. So pray for the time to be with them and that learning will be a joy when you are together.

As your children get older, they probably won't be quite so motivated to learn. This poses another opportunity for you to pray for them, to talk things like their education and schoolwork over with God. What generally motivates you to do something? Usually it's knowing why something is important, right? If you have a reason, you're more motivated to get the job done. So again, pray that you can help your children understand the importance of learning in general and their schoolwork specifically. Sit down and explain God's desire that we do all things well, including schoolwork, that it's our way of preparing for the future—for a future of serving God and for the future He has in mind for each of us. In other words, that's the "why."

So in all your praying, pray for your children's willingness to work and desire to do well. Then follow-up to see how they're doing with their schoolwork. Let them know by your involvement that you love them

> *No work is too small to be done well.*

and care how they're doing. And as a reminder, also pray for wisdom for them—and for you—as together you assist each child in determining the way he or she should go practically and vocationally.

For decades I prayed for my daughters' teachers. It's a must for a mom after God's own heart, whether your kids are in secular or private schools. Pray for God's saving grace for their teachers. Pray for your children to be a consistent witness of their faith in God. And if your child is in a Christian school, pray for their teachers and their walk with God. Also pray about what their teachers are teaching. School is a huge part of every child's life, and it makes up a huge part of your life and your prayer life. And if you're homeschooling? Pray for your diligence as you faithfully prepare and for your children to hear what you have to say as a teacher. Your prayers need to cover every educational scenario. Pray the content of Colossians 3:23-24:

> Lord, whatever [your child's name] does, including his (her) schoolwork, motivate him (her) to do it heartily, as to the Lord and not to men.

5. Pray for Your Child's Church Involvement

Amazingly, when children are little, they want to be involved in whatever you're involved in, especially at church. But as they age, it takes a little more than that. That's why, from an early age, Jim and I prayed for the salvation of our two children. Without the indwelling Holy Spirit, a child will become less and less interested in church. So again, a relationship with Christ as Savior is the starting point for your prayers.

And while you're praying for God to open young hearts, keep taking them to church. This will help develop in them the pattern of going to church. As parents, we made it a habit for our family to attend every worship service at church. We also made sure that our girls participated in every activity for their age group, including camps. We sacrificed whatever it took, whether time or money or inconvenience. We didn't want them to miss out on any and every opportunity for God's Spirit to work in their young and impressionable lives.

You and I can—and should—pray long and hard about our child's participation at church. But we should also remember that their involvement is influenced by our involvement, especially as they get older. Pray for their Bible clubs, church activities, youth groups, service opportunities, and camps. Treat them as being even more important than their schoolwork. And put their Sunday school teachers or youth pastors on their individual daily prayer lists too. These are important people in your kids' lives, and you'll want to pray earnestly for them as they teach your children about God and their walk with Him.

When it comes to your children and their involvement and instruction at church, pray along with 2 Peter 3:18 and Ephesians 4:15:

> Lord, may [your child's name] grow in the grace and knowledge of our Lord and Savior

Jesus Christ. May he (she) grow up in all
things into Him who is the head—Christ.

Think about prayer for a moment. As we've journeyed
together through these ten ways to love our children,
there has been much for us to *do*. For instance, we are to
take time to nurture our own heart. Then we are to
teach, talk, tell, train, and take care of our children. And
we are also to take them to church, teach them to pray,
and do our best. That's a lot of *doing*.

But in this chapter, with this most important way to
love your children, in this utterly heavenly category, we
don't *do*. Instead we *pray*. It's spiritual labor. It's the
mighty ministry we perform when we talk to God about
our children. It's the time when we plead, supplicate,
importune, appeal, and ask God to work in our children's
lives. It's when we come boldly before our God and His
throne of grace and talk over our concerns about our
children with Him.

So who is a mom after God's own heart? She's a mom
who's devoted to preaching and praying. No matter what
your children's ages, you will be teaching your children
the scriptures that will train them for God and guide
their lives. (This is the preaching part of the formula.)
And, of course, you are going to be talking to your child
about God at any and every opportunity. (This might be

considered to be even *more* preaching.) But most of all, you are going to be talking to God about each of your precious ones. And this is the praying part. And, mom, we do it with all of our heart...for life! It's what a mom after God's own heart does.

From a Dad's Heart

In the first chapter of this book, Elizabeth suggested that, if it was appropriate and your husband was interested, you might invite him to read my "Dad" pages. I have written these sections to suggest how you can help your husband to assist you in raising your children. Prayer is one of the most special ways both of you can love your kids. Prayer is not like feeding or clothing or sheltering your children. But prayer is as important or more important than anything physical you can do for them. Prayer is also a unique opportunity for a dad. As a Christian, God has ordained that your husband be the spiritual head of the family. Part of that responsibility involves praying for you and the children.

When I think of a parent or a father in the Bible who prayed for his children, I immediately think of Job in the Old Testament. I know I mentioned him before, but if your husband is interested in having a model to follow for his own prayers for the children, ask him to read Job 1:1-5. As you or he reads, you'll see Job's prayers as a parent involved three elements:

♡ First, Job prayed with *focus*. He probably prayed for many other things, but in the opening verses of the book that bears his name, God wants us to know that Job's family was a priority for his prayer time. He had seven sons and prayed for each one by name (Job 1:4-5).

♡ Next, Job prayed with *frequency*. He didn't pray for his children on a hit-and-miss basis. He prayed "regularly" (verse 5).

♡ Finally, Job prayed with *fervency*. He rose up early to pray for each of his children. Job was concerned for their spiritual condition. His thoughts centered around their conduct. Job reasoned in his mind, "Perhaps my children have sinned and cursed God in their hearts" (verse 5 NIV). So he prayed.

Job provides a model for all parents—especially dads—to follow when it comes to praying for our children. However, you, as a mom, should never fail to pray for your children. Don't assume your husband is praying for them. Pray that he is, but be sure you are praying. And if you can, pray together with your husband for the children.

As you can see, there is always much to pray for your husband too, for the father of your children. Pray for his sensitivity toward the children. Pray that he will assume his position as spiritual head of the family if he isn't already doing that now. Also pray that your husband will read these few verses about Job's prayers for his children. Obviously, if your husband isn't a Christian, he won't have a great desire to pray, so pray for him to become a Christian. As I've heard Elizabeth encourage women so many times, "the effective, fervent prayer of a righteous *[wife and mom]* avails much" (James 5:16).

Little Choices That Reap Big Blessings

1. Create prayer pages for your children.

Make one general page and one personal page for each child. Then begin recording your concerns. We only covered "The Top Five" in this chapter, but obviously there are many more concerns we moms have for our precious ones. So make your own lists...and pray, pray, pray. As God's goodness and grace are revealed in answers and your pages are filled with His will concerning your prayers, file them away. For me, these pages were placed in a file folder. Then, as the filled pages continue to come along, they soon required an entire file drawer for storage!

As the years of mothering pass, even the dark and baffling ones, be sure to go back and revisit the answers to previous prayers. Be blessed again and again. Have your faith strengthened over and over as you remember each situation and how God worked in your life and in the life of each child. Give Him thanks for His goodness and faithfulness.

2. Enlist the prayer support of others.

Do you have godly relatives or very close friends? Who better to pray along with you at every stage of your child's spiritual and physical development than a grandparent, or a special aunt, or a trusted and longtime friend? But do be careful not to be too specific about some areas of your child's life. You don't want to betray the trust of your child and permanently mar another person's opinion and memories of your child.

3. Set aside some time each day to pray for each child.

Let me ask you a question: If you aren't praying for your child, who is? Maybe a godly dad or a godly grandparent? But it's possible that on any given day, you are the only one praying for your child. Please don't miss a day. Your child needs your prayers. Do you have ten minutes? That's a fairly "little choice."

But also be aware that the more children you have, the greater the time commitment will become. I met one faithful grandmother who committed to pray 10 minutes when the first grandchild came along. Now she has 24 grandchildren and is praying 4 hours a day! Is praying for your child important to you? If it is, then you'll find the time...no matter how many children you have.

4. Pray with each child every day.

This great privilege usually comes at bedtime. Ask each child privately about his or her day. How did things go? Any problem relationships? Together pray for what happened today and what's going to happen tomorrow. Don't send your children to bed without prayer. These precious opportunities will soon be gone. Take advantage of these times to teach your children the importance of prayer as together you see how God is going to answer your combined prayers.

5. Pray for your child's schedule.

This won't be too difficult for a two- or nine-year-old, but a 16- or 17-year-old's life and schedule can get pretty hectic. By knowing their schedules (which you found out while you prayed and tucked them in the night before—and yes, I mean your teens too!), you will know how to be praying as events unfold throughout the day. Then ask how things went when the children return home at the end of the day. And don't forget to seal the report with yet another prayer.

6. Find scriptures to pray.

I've shared some of the prayers I prayed for my children—and still pray!—that use scripture. Please help yourself to them. Write them on 3″ x 5″ cards and carry them with you...everywhere. When you are reading your Bible or attending church or Bible study, keep your ears open to other scriptures to pray. Jesus prayed for His own in John 17. You can draw rich scripture text here from the heart of the Master Pray-er and Lover of our souls. And Paul prayed for his disciples. The epistles contain multiple prayers from his heart that you can use for your little and big "disciples." Colossians 1:9-14 is a great place to start. When you pray using scripture, you can have confidence that you are praying according to God's will...and that He hears you (1 John 5:14).

Making the Choices That Count

Making the Choices That Count

In all your ways acknowledge Him,
and He shall direct your paths.

PROVERBS 3:6

Have you ever been at a place in your life where you began to think that the churning of the turbulent sea of life had finally calmed (or at least was calmer!), and you just might sail into some calm water? Well, that's the way I felt just after we became a Christian family. Jim had a good job. Our children were healthy. We had just returned from our first church service with brand-new Bibles in hand. We at last had purpose in our lives and a direction for our family. As a unit, we wanted to follow Jesus.

235

That was on a glorious Sunday.

Then came Monday. That's the day Jim came home from work and informed me he wanted to quit his job, go back to school, and prepare to enter the ministry.

Needless to say, that churning, turbulent sea started right back up again! But this time something was different. I now had the Holy Spirit to help me (you know, with things like patience and self-control!). My immediate response was, "But what about all that we've worked so hard for up to this point—a nice house, furniture that's paid for, your job advancement, medical coverage, a regular paycheck?" Obviously I was only thinking of myself. But it wasn't long before I came around to God's plan for our family...and His peace. Together Jim and I made the choice to basically sell all and follow Jesus. We made the choice to leave everything behind and follow God's call on Jim's life to go into the ministry.

Now I am not sharing this to say you should do as we did. No, God leads each person, husband, wife, mom, and family in different ways and in different directions. I share it to illustrate the impact one choice—just *one* choice!—to follow God's leading had on my life and the lives of those in my family. That choice set in motion the most remarkable 30 years. And that's just one of many choices (hopefully right ones) we've made during the following decades as we attempted with all our hearts to follow Christ. And choices are never made in a vacuum. Yes, they affect us personally, but they also affect others...like our children. This childhood saying underscores the direction of our little choices: "Little choices determine habit; habit carves and molds character, which makes the big decisions."

The Results of One Little Wrong Choice

Abraham, in the Old Testament, faced a problem...but it was a good problem. You see, God had blessed. As Abraham and his nephew, Lot, wandered throughout the land of Canaan in answer to God's call on their lives, they amassed herds and flocks. These herds were a sign of wealth for nomads like Abraham and Lot. But the land could not sustain both men and their herds (Genesis 13:5-7). What to do was Abraham's dilemma.

Graciously, Abraham decided to allow his nephew to choose between two directions and two different types of land for his herds, herdsmen, and family. Abraham explained to Lot, "If you take the left, then I will go to the right; or, if you go to the right, then I will go to the left" (verse 9). In one direction the land was "well watered...like the garden of the LORD" (verse 10). The Bible doesn't say, but the land in the other direction had to be less desirable in its desert setting.

By offering Lot his choice, Abraham was risking the first and best choice, a choice rightly his as the elder. And sure enough, the nephew took advantage of what seemed to be a good business decision: Herds need grass and water to survive, right? So he chose the well-watered, garden environment.

History is made every time you make a decision.

Unfortunately, however, this wasn't the best choice spiritually. Lot separated himself from the godly Abraham and moved his herds and his family to the green pastures near Sodom and Gomorrah. (Do these towns sound familiar?) In the end, Lot's choice—a little choice between going right or going left—had disastrous consequences. God judged these two cities filled with wicked people, but spared the lives of Lot and his family. But in the process of the purging, Lot lost everything—his herds, his wife, and eventually his children, so to speak, when his daughters' lives were ruined as they lost their moral and sexual purity (Genesis 19:1-29). Why all of this devastation? Because of one little wrong choice.

Making the Right Choices

We've been talking throughout this book about becoming moms after God's own heart. We started by looking into the depths of our own hearts to make sure we were truly desiring to follow God's design for us as His moms. Now it's time to put that love and desire for our children to work and make a few more choices—hopefully the good, better, and best choices—the choices that really count.

Throughout time, God's moms have been making right choices—and sometimes hard choices. For instance,

♡ Moses' mother risked her own life to make a choice not to follow the king's edict. Instead of killing her baby as ordered, she held onto him and preserved his life (Exodus 1:22–2:10).

♡ King David's great-great-grandmother, Rahab-the-harlot (Matthew 1:5), risked her life and made a choice to hide Joshua's spies rather than turn them in to the king (Joshua 2).

♡ Samuel's mother, Hannah, made a choice to follow through on her vow to give up her only son to God's service (1 Samuel 1–2).

Like these moms in the Bible, not all of the choices you make will be easy. Some, in fact, may be costly to your own personal ambitions. And many of your decisions may go against the culture of our day. Others will require more of your already nonexistent time. But in the long run, and in God's economy, they will be the right choices—God's choices—choices that will count for your family now, in times to come, and also in eternity.

As we begin to wrap up our time together as moms, please make the choices that follow a matter of prayer. Talk them over with God. Talk them through with your husband. This list is in no way exhaustive. It does, however, reflect the kinds of choices every mom is faced with. As you lay your heart and your life and your family before God, He will lead you to make the right choices. For He is the One who promises "I will instruct you and teach you in the way you should go; I will counsel you and watch over you" (Psalm 32:8 NIV). Indeed, the Lord will direct your steps, and "he will be [your] guide even to the end" (Proverbs 16:9; Psalm 48:14 NIV).

Choose to Put Your Personal Dreams on Hold

Put *your* dreams, your career and educational goals, the development of your hobbies and abilities on hold. You don't need to kill your dreams. Just keep them in the background while you live out your role of mom at warp speed. If a pocket of time comes along, then you can take a class or attend a special workshop and away you go, taking one step at a time.

Several chapters back I shared how I chose to drop the master's degree program and focus my attention on my home and my family. In that choice I was, in effect, determining to be the best mom and wife I could be...and those two points of concentration became a full-time commitment.

But as I slipped into the routine of mothering and got more organized at home, I became aware of certain times in the day when I could spend time reading and studying. So I enrolled in a Moody Bible Institute correspondence course.[1] I still remember how I would finish a course and eagerly wait for my grade. Then I would sign up for the next class in the series and nibble away. I also started memorizing Bible verses at those odd times during the day, such as when the girls were napping or while I watched them play on the swings and gym equipment at the park.

> *Life is not the result of dreams dreamed, but of choices made.*

In time, in a number of years, my dream came true. I completed every Bible course offered. No, I didn't get a degree. That's not what I wanted. But I got what I dreamed of—a working knowledge and understanding of the Bible, all accomplished in snatches of time here and there.

What are your dreams? Own them, write them down, pray about them...but manage them. As the wisdom of Ecclesiastes teaches us, "to everything there is a season, a time for every purpose under heaven" (Ecclesiastes 3:1). Several specifics are scattered throughout verses 2-8: "There is...a time to plant...a time to build up...a time to gain...a time to love." In other words, timing is important. We are to concentrate on doing the right things at the right time in our lives. "Earthly pursuits are good in their proper place and time, but unprofitable when pursued as the chief goal."[2] Everything in its own season!

Choose to Put First People First

Family is first. That's what Titus 2:3-5 teaches us. Here we read that the older women are to teach the younger women to #1—"love their husbands" and #2—"love their children." This is God's divine order. So choose to give the first people in your life the first fruits of your time, love, and energy.

When it comes to priority efforts, I can't help but think of Moses' mom (Jochebed) and Samuel's mom (Hannah). They knew—and practiced—their priorities. Each of these "moms after God's own heart" had only a handful of years—about three—to pour a lifetime of love and godly instruction into their little boys. And then Jochebed turned little Moses over to Pharaoh's daughter to be raised in Pharaoh's palace. And Hannah turned little Samuel over to be raised under the tutelage of the priest Eli. What if...they hadn't given their all to their little guys during the time they did have? What if...they hadn't gotten up every single morning and poured their all into eager hearts? What if...they hadn't been there? What if...they had been consumed with other pursuits? What if...they hadn't taken each day as a mom seriously? What if...?

But they were...and they did! And you and I—and all of mankind—are the better for it. These two boys grew to be men who served God mightily and helped change the world.

Choose to Be Mentored

Here's another bit of advice from Titus 2. Verses 3 and 4 say "the older women" are to "admonish the young women to love...their children." God's plan for us as Christian moms is that we be learning from those moms who have gone before us, who are taking their mommy-hood seriously, who can show us the ropes, who can encourage us in our roles as moms.

One day, when I was reading through the galleys of Jim's book on the apostle Paul's mentoring ministry, I learned the history of the term "mentor." Legend has it that the man Mentor was the tutor of Telemachus, whose father Odysseus left home for almost a decade to fight in the Trojan War. Mentor, in essence, raised Telemachus and taught and trained him for life. Thus a mentor is one who tutors, teaches, and trains.

I've probably stated in most of my books that God gave me the gift of many mentors during the years when I was getting grounded in the Christian faith. Those wonderful women pointed me in a biblical direction, helped accelerate my growth in Christ, and provided models of what a godly woman, wife, and mom looks like. As one who's benefited from a mentor, my advice is choose to be mentored.

How? First, pray. Then look around for an "older woman," a mentor, to disciple you in your different roles, "mom" being one of them. Who seems friendly? Who takes an interest in you as a young mom? Who's got her mothering act together...somewhat, anyway? Pray again, and then approach her with your Number One question or problem at the moment. You can do this in a few minutes on the phone, you can talk with her briefly in the church lobby, or maybe it will work out for you to meet for a while, even if it's with your children and hers at the park or at a fast-food restaurant with a play area. Open yourself up and ask her for help. Seek advice. Then ask her the next question...and the next...and *viola!* you have a mentor!

Another way to be mentored is by joining a moms or MOPS (Moms of Preschoolers) group. MOPS International is a well-organized Christian association that has older mentors and mother-figures who assist young moms. One of my daughters is actively involved in one of these groups, and she constantly shares with me what she's learning. It's an important lifeline for her and the other moms.

Choose to Read Proverbs

I'm sure you've noticed that throughout this book I've often referred to the book of Proverbs. Proverbs is one of the wisdom books of the Bible, and it gives us wisdom for knowing how to deal with relationships, including relationships with our children. I was challenged as a new believer to read one chapter of the book of Proverbs each day. Over the years this practice has saturated my heart, soul, and mind with God's directions on how I should interact with people, my children included.

> *Your level of maturity is in direct proportion to your ability to make wise decisions.*

For instance, are you looking for wisdom regarding the daily opportunities your kids give you to discipline and train them? Proverbs has the answers to your every quandary. For example, I found these principles that I call "The Three C's" when I needed to know how to treat certain common problems of dissension between siblings.

C-asting lots—helps settle disputes
(Proverbs 18:18)

C-orrecting—helps reduce tension
(Proverbs 29:17)

C-asting out the instigator—helps restore
peace (Proverbs 22:10)

Read Proverbs yourself. Receive its instruction, gain God's wisdom, and put it to work in your home. Then turn around and pass it on to the next generation. Help your children love and appreciate the book of Proverbs as much as you do. It will equip them with wisdom for life!

Choose to Study the Moms in the Bible

Oh, is this ever one of my passions! I have books and books on my library shelves about the women of the Bible. Reading about their lives as moms has given me encouragement since my girls were in diapers! These moms continue to teach me valuable lessons and principles as a mom—some in the positive and, unfortunately, some in the negative.

Reading about their lives brings us face-to-face with the great mothers of the faith—Eve, Sarah, Rebekah, Jochebed, Samson's mother, Naomi, Hannah, the Proverbs 31 mom, Elizabeth, and Mary. What an education to see how they handled the everyday trials and challenges all moms encounter! And what a treat to see how they loved their children—how they taught them, talked to them, told them about God, took care of them, trained them, talked to God about them, and tried their best! And what straightforward instruction—from God's Word to your heart!

As I prayed about how to end not only this section of the book, but the book itself, I reserved this "choice" for last—*Choose your attitude*. Why? Because it's something you can do right away. It's a little choice you can make in your heart right this minute. And I promise you, it's a little choice that reaps b-i-g blessings...daily and forever!

Being an unbelieving mom was a hard and hopeless time in my life. With two little babies only 13 months apart, I was Old Mother Hubbard—I was only 25, and I already had so many children that I didn't know what to do! And then, as a new Christian mom, I began to understand my role and accept my responsibility. I also learned that the Bible considers children to be "a heritage from the LORD" and "a reward" (Psalm 127:3), that to have children is to be blessed by God.

So I embraced God's exalted role of "mother." And I tackled my attitude. As one scholar advised, the language of the Bible is calling us as Christians "to change our attitudes and actions toward" our children and our mothering.[3] According to God's Word, I, as one of His moms, was to exhibit and live by—and live out—certain attitudes of heart.

What kind of mom does God want me—and you—to be? Answer: One who carries out her mothering with these attitudes of heart and in these ways:

Heartily—Whatever you do, including being a mom, do it heartily as to the Lord (Colossians 3:23).

Faithfully—Be faithful in all things, especially in your role of mom (1 Timothy 3:11).

Willingly—Do your work as a mom willingly, with both hands and your whole heart (Proverbs 31:15).

Excellently—Many moms do well, but seek to excel them all (Proverbs 31:29).

Joyfully—Rejoice always, no matter what your job as mom calls for (1 Thessalonians 5:16).

Prayerfully—Pray without ceasing while you're doing everything being a mom after God's own heart requires (1 Thessalonians 5:17).

Thankfully—In everything, especially in being a mom, give thanks, for this is the will of God in Christ Jesus for you (1 Thessalonians 5:18).

May you, my friend, be this mom—a mom after God's own heart...the mom you want to be.

From a Dad's Heart

It's been said of Billy Graham's mother that she was a simple dairy farmer's wife who never led a committee or a Bible study at church or made any outstanding public contributions. Her contribution at home, however, had eternal consequences. Billy's mother prayed reverently for 17 years until his salvation. Then she spent the next 50 years of her life praying for Billy and his ministry. Mrs. Graham chose to focus her attention on her home and family. Obviously this one choice reaped eternal dividends.

My mom also focused her attention on being the best wife and mom she could be. There were those wayward years when she may have been a little discouraged by my choices and conduct, but mom never gave up on me. And, by God's grace and mom's persistent prayers, I finally came around spiritually. Then she prayed and encouraged me until the day she died, even moving as a widow to live near me and my family so she could be of help with our family and with our ministry efforts. She was an excellent mom and grandmom, and her death left a real vacuum in our lives.

Choices are a funny thing. No one can make your choices for you. What you choose to focus your time and life on is ultimately between you and God. I know I speak for Elizabeth also when I urge you to seek God's wisdom and the counsel of your husband and of godly men and women as you make your choices about how you live out your role of being a mom.

As a dad looking at my family today and the role Elizabeth played in the lives of our daughters, I wonder how it would have been if she hadn't made the choice to focus on our children. What if...

> ...she hadn't been there during those preschool years when the majority of foundational learning takes place? If she hadn't been there to read Bible stories, correct bad habits, and personally ensure that our daughters' little minds were being filled with the things of God rather than the things of the world?

> ...she hadn't been there when, like so many dads who hold down 50-plus-hours-a-week jobs, my job called for long hours and nights or weekends away from home, when I was gone weeks

at a time on mission trips and at leadership conferences?

...she hadn't been there during those teen years when hormones and emotions were running wild? If she hadn't been there to send our kids off to school and be there at the door waiting for them with a sandwich and a Coke and a listening ear?

...she hadn't been there for them during those young adult years when decisions were being made as to career preparation and life-mates? If she hadn't been available to the girls anytime of the day or night when they just needed to talk?

...she hadn't been there when the girls started their own homes and the babies started arriving? If she hadn't been ready, willing, and able to jump on a plane each time a new grandchild was born and take care of both baby and mom until our daughters were able to resume normal activities? And even what if she hadn't been available to listen to the cries of a disheartened daughter after a miscarriage?

But Elizabeth was there, and she has been for more than 30 years. All of the precious moments represented were made possible partly because of the choices of one mom who focused her life and energies on two little girls who grew up to have seven little people of their own.

What choices are you making? And are there any moments you are missing because of some decisions you've made? It's not too late to change course. I'm not here to put a guilt trip on you. I know you love your children. And I know you want to be a good mom because you've made it to the last page of a book on being God's kind of mom. I also know you and your husband have goals that you've set together.

One day you and your husband will look back at the results of the choices you've made. What a blessing it will be to see that you sought God's wisdom as you made your decisions, that you were truly a mom after God's own heart! Congratulations on your desire to raise children after God's own heart and on your calling as a mom. It's a high and privileged one!

QUIET TIMES CALENDAR

Jan.	Feb.	Mar.	Apr.	May	June
1	1	1	1	1	1
2	2	2	2	2	2
3	3	3	3	3	3
4	4	4	4	4	4
5	5	5	5	5	5
6	6	6	6	6	6
7	7	7	7	7	7
8	8	8	8	8	8
9	9	9	9	9	9
10	10	10	10	10	10
11	11	11	11	11	11
12	12	12	12	12	12
13	13	13	13	13	13
14	14	14	14	14	14
15	15	15	15	15	15
16	16	16	16	16	16
17	17	17	17	17	17
18	18	18	18	18	18
19	19	19	19	19	19
20	20	20	20	20	20
21	21	21	21	21	21
22	22	22	22	22	22
23	23	23	23	23	23
24	24	24	24	24	24
25	25	25	25	25	25
26	26	26	26	26	26
27	27	27	27	27	27
28	28	28	28	28	28
29	29	29	29	29	29
30		30	30	30	30
31		31		31	

July	Aug.	Sept.	Oct.	Nov.	Dec.
1	1	1	1	1	1
2	2	2	2	2	2
3	3	3	3	3	3
4	4	4	4	4	4
5	5	5	5	5	5
6	6	6	6	6	6
7	7	7	7	7	7
8	8	8	8	8	8
9	9	9	9	9	9
10	10	10	10	10	10
11	11	11	11	11	11
12	12	12	12	12	12
13	13	13	13	13	13
14	14	14	14	14	14
15	15	15	15	15	15
16	16	16	16	16	16
17	17	17	17	17	17
18	18	18	18	18	18
19	19	19	19	19	19
20	20	20	20	20	20
21	21	21	21	21	21
22	22	22	22	22	22
23	23	23	23	23	23
24	24	24	24	24	24
25	25	25	25	25	25
26	26	26	26	26	26
27	27	27	27	27	27
28	28	28	28	28	28
29	29	29	29	29	29
30	30	30	30	30	30
31	31		31		31

Notes

Focusing on the Heart

1. W.E. Vine, *Vine's Expository Dictionary of Old and New Testament Words* (Nashville: Thomas Nelson Publishers, 1997), p. 537.
2. William MacDonald, *Enjoying the Proverbs* (Kansas City, KS: Walterick Publishers, 1982), p. 31.
3. Vine, *Vine's Expository Dictionary,* p. 537.
4. Michael Kendrick and Daryl Lucas, *365 Life Lessons from Bible People* (Wheaton, IL: Tyndale House Publishers, Inc., 1996), p. 92.
5. Ivor Powell, *David: His Life and Times — A Biographical Commentary* (Grand Rapids, MI: Kregel Publications, 1990), p. 24.
6. Ibid., p. 27.
7. Charles F. Pfeiffer and Everett F. Harrison, *The Wycliffe Bible Commentary* (Chicago: Moody Press, 1990), p. 773.
8. John MacArthur, *The MacArthur Study Bible* (Nashville: Word Bibles, 1997), p. 1227.
9. Ibid., p. 1662.
10. Kendrick and Lucas, *365 Life Lessons,* p. 355.

1—Take Time to Nurture Your Heart

1. See Elizabeth George, *A Woman's High Calling* (Eugene, OR: Harvest House Publishers, 2001), pp. 168-81.
2. Elizabeth George, *A Mom After God's Own Heart Growth and Study Guide* (Eugene, OR: Harvest House Publishers, 2005).
3. Charles F. Pfeiffer and Everett F. Harrison, *The Wycliffe Bible Commentary* (Chicago: Moody Press, 1990), p. 164.
4. Matthew Henry, *Matthew Henry's Commentary on the Whole Bible* (Peabody, MA: Hendrickson Publishers, 2003), p. 244.
5. *Life Application Study Bible* (Wheaton, IL: Tyndale House Publishers, Inc., 1996), p. 269.
6. *The One Year Bible* (Wheaton, IL: Tyndale House Publishers, Inc., 1986).

2—Teach Your Children God's Word

1. "The Soul of a Child," in Eleanor Doan, *Speaker's Sourcebook* (Grand Rapids, MI: Zondervan Publishing House, 1988), p. 51.

255

2. Tedd Tripp, *Shepherding a Child's Heart* (Wapallopen, PA: Shepherd Press, 1995), pp. 29-32.

3. G.M. Mackie, *Bible Manners and Customs* (Old Tappan, NJ: Fleming H. Revell Company, n.d.), p. 158.

4. Information drawn from Matthew Henry, *Matthew Henry's Commentary on the Whole Bible*, (Peabody, MA: Hendrickson Publishers, 2003), p. 244.

5. Mackie, *Bible Manners and Customs*, p. 154.

6. E. Margaret Clarkson.

7. Mackie, *Bible Manners and Customs*, p. 159.

8. Curtis Vaughan, *The Word—The Bible from 26 Translations* (Gulfport, MS: Mathis Publishers, Inc., 1991), p. 339.

9. "The Heart of a Child," in Doan, *Speaker's Sourcebook*, p. 52.

3—Talk to Your Children About God

1. See Proverbs 12:23-24, for example.

2. Richard W. DeHaan and Henry G. Bosch, *Our Daily Bread Favorites* (Grand Rapids, MI: Zondervan Publishing House, 1971), February 3.

3. George Barna survey results, *Transforming Children into Spiritual Champions* (Ventura, CA: Regal Books Gospel Light, 2003), p. 35.

4. Hans Finzel, *Help! I'm a Baby Boomer* (Wheaton, IL: Victor Books, 1989), p. 105.

5. Sid Buzzell, *The Leadership Bible* (Grand Rapids, MI: Zondervan Publishing House, 1998), p. 207.

4—Tell Your Children About Jesus

1. George Barna survey results, *Transforming Children into Spiritual Champions* (Ventura, CA: Regal Books Gospel Light, 2003), p. 41.

2. Elgin S. Moyer, *Who Was Who in Church History* (New Canaan, CT: Keats Publishing, Inc.), 1974, p. 22.

3. Jerry Noble, cited in Albert M. Wells, Jr., *Inspiring Quotations—Contemporary & Classical* (Nashville: Thomas Nelson Publishers, 1988), p. 82.

4. Moyer, *Who Was Who*, p. 293.

5. Paul Lee Tan, *Encyclopedia of 7700 Illustrations* (Winona Lake, IN: BMH Books, 1979), p. 851.

5—Train Your Children in God's Ways

1. Elizabeth George, *God's Wisdom for Little Girls: Virtues and Fun from Proverbs 31*, with paintings by Judy Luenebrink (Eugene, OR: Harvest House Publishers, 2000).

2. William MacDonald, *Enjoying the Proverbs*, quoting Jay Adams, *Competent to Counsel* (Grand Rapids, MI: Baker Book House, 1970), Walterick Publishers, P.O. Box 2216, Kansas City, KS 66110, 1982), p. 120.

3. See Proverbs 13:24; 23:13-14; 29:15,17.

4. Eleanor Doan, *Speaker's Sourcebook* (Grand Rapids, MI: Zondervan Publishing House, 1988), p. 48.

5. Benjamin R. DeJong, *Uncle Ben's Quotebook* (Grand Rapids, MI: Baker Book House, 1977), p. 142, no author's name given.

6. Heart to Heart Program cited in Doan, *Speaker's Sourcebook*, p. 49.

7. Horace Bushnell in Doan, *Speaker's Sourcebook*, p. 49.

8. The New American Bible and James Moffatt, A New Translation of the Bible, respectively, cited in Curtis Vaughan, *The Word—The Bible from 26 Translations* (Gulfport, MS: Mathis Publishers, Inc., 1991), p. 1221.

9. Robert Jamieson, A.R. Fausset, and David Brown, *Commentary on the Whole Bible* (Grand Rapids, MI: Zondervan Publishing House, 1971), p. 470.

10. Ralph Wardlaw, *Lectures on the Book of Proverbs*, vol. III (Minneapolis: Klock & Klock Christian Publishers, Inc., 1982 reprint), p. 38.

11. Jim George, *A Young Man After God's Own Heart* (Eugene OR: Harvest House Publishers, 2005), p. 86.

12. Bruce Barton, *Life Application Bible Commentary—Ephesians* (Wheaton, IL: Tyndale House Publishers, Inc., 1996), p. 122.

13. J. David Branon, as cited in Roy B. Zuck, *The Speaker's Quote Book* (Grand Rapids, MI: Kregel Publications, 1977), p. 51.

14. "Home Life" in Doan, *Speaker's Sourcebook*, p. 50.

6 — Take Care of Your Children

1. Pat Ennis and Lisa Tatlock, *Designing a Lifestyle that Pleases God* (Chicago: Moody Publishers, 2004), pp. 113-15.

2. Tiger's Milk® is a nutrition bar loaded with 18 vitamins and minerals and 11 grams of protein.

3. Curtis Vaughan, *The Word—The Bible from 26 Translations* ASV (Gulfport, MS: Mathis Publishers, Inc., 1991), p. 1246.

4. Alice Gray, Steve Stephens, John Van Diest, *Lists to Live By for Every Caring Family* (Sisters, OR: Multnomah Publishers, 2001), pp. 96 and 110.

5. Ibid., p. 19.

6. Elizabeth George, *Beautiful in God's Eyes—The Treasures of the Proverbs 31 Woman* (Eugene, OR: Harvest House Publishers, 1998).

7. See Proverbs 1:10-19; 5:1-11; 7:1-27.

7—Take Your Children to Church

1. "A Child's Ten Commandments to Parents," by Dr. Kevin Leman, from *Getting the Best Out of Your Kids* (Eugene, OR: Harvest House Publishers, 1992). Quoted in Alice Gray, Steve Stephens, John Van Diest, *Lists to Live By for Every Caring Family* (Sisters, OR: Multnomah Publishers, 2001), p. 130.

2. Robert Jamieson, A.R. Fausset, and David Brown, *Commentary on the Whole Bible* (Grand Rapids, MI: Zondervan Publishing House, 1971), p. 1429.

3. Drawn from Richard Mayhue, *Seeking God* (Fearn, Great Britain: Christian Focus Publications, 2000), p. 148.

4. Bruce B. Barton, *Life Application Bible Commentary—Mark* (Wheaton, IL: Tyndale House Publishers, Inc., 1994), p. 285.

5. George Barna survey results, *Transforming Children into Spiritual Champions* (Ventura, CA: Regal Books Gospel Light, 2003), p. 41.

6. Joe White, Jim Weidmann, *Spiritual Mentoring of Teens* (Wheaton, IL: Tyndale House Publishers, 2001), p. 49.

7. Paul Lee Tan, *Encyclopedia of 7700 Illustrations* (Winona Lake, IN: BMH Books, 1979), p. 844.

8. Mary Louise Kitsen, "Generations of Excuses," reprinted by permission.

8—Teach Your Children to Pray

1. Herbert Lockyer, *All the Prayers of the Bible* (Grand Rapids, MI: Zondervan Publishing House, 1973), p. 64.

2. *Matthew Henry's Commentary on the Whole Bible* (Hendrickson Publishers, Inc., 2003), p. 383.

3. D.L. Moody, *Thoughts from My Library* (Grand Rapids, MI: Baker Book House, 1979), p. 122.

4. "This I Carry with Me Always," *Christian Parenting Today*, May/June 1993, p. 23.

5. Stanley High, *Billy Graham* (New York: McGraw Hill, 1956), p. 106.

6. George Barna survey results, *Transforming Children into Spiritual Champions* (Ventura, CA: Regal Books, published from Gospel Light, 2003), p. 35.

7. For your teen girls, see Elizabeth George, *A Young Woman After God's Own Heart* and *A Young Woman's Call to Prayer* (Eugene, OR: Harvest House Publishers, 2003 and 2005). For your teen boys, see Jim George, *A Young Man After God's Own Heart* (Eugene, OR: Harvest House Publishers, 2005).

8. *The Prayers of Susanna Wesley*, ed. and arr. by W.L. Doughty (Grand Rapids, MI: Zondervan Publishing House, Clarion Classics, 1984), p. 46.

9. Arthur Bennett, ed., *The Valley of Vision* (Carlisle, PA: The Banner of Truth Trust, 1999).

10. Joe White and Jim Weidmann, *Spiritual Mentoring of Teens* (Wheaton, IL: Tyndale House Publishers, 2001), pp. 76, 35.

9—Try Your Best

1. Elisabeth Elliot, *The Shaping of a Christian Family* (Nashville, TN: Thomas Nelson Publishers, 1991), pp. 95.

2. Judith Warner, "Mommy Madness," *Newsweek, Inc.,* 2005, quoting from *Perfect Madness* (New York: Riverhead Books, 2005).

3. Elizabeth George, *Loving God with All Your Mind* (Eugene, OR: Harvest House Publishers, 1994/2005).

4. See especially Elizabeth George, *A Woman After God's Own Heart®* and *A Wife After God's Own Heart* (Eugene, OR: Harvest House Publishers, 1997 and 2004).

5. Judith Warner, "Mommy Madness," *Newsweek, Inc.,* 2005, February 21, 2005, www.msnbc.msn.com/id/6959880/site/newsweek, quoting from her book *Perfect Madness* (England: Riverhead Books, a division of Penguin Group (USA) Inc., 2005).

10—Talk to God About Your Children

1. John MacArthur, *The MacArthur Study Bible* (Nashville: Word Publishing, 1997), p. 877.

Making the Choices that Count

1. Moody Bible Institute Distance Learning, 820 North LaSalle Blvd., Chicago, IL 60610, 1-800-758-6352 or check out www.mdlc.moody.edu.

2. John MacArthur, *The MacArthur Study Bible* (Nashville, TN: Word Publishing, 1997), p. 929.

3. Gene A. Getz, *The Measure of a Woman* (Glendale, CA: Regal-Gospel Light Publications, 1977), p. 73.

Personal Notes

Personal Notes

Personal Notes

Personal Notes

Personal Notes

Personal Notes

If you've benefited from *A Mom After God's Own Heart,* you'll want the companion volume

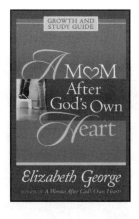

A *Mom After God's Own Heart*
Growth
and
Study Guide

This guide offers additional scriptures, thought-provoking questions, reflective studies, and personal and practical applications that will help you be the best mom you can be.

This growth and study guide is perfect for both personal and group use.

A Mom After God's Own Heart Growth and Study Guide is available at your local Christian bookstore or can be ordered from:

Elizabeth George
PO Box 2879
Belfair, WA 98528
Toll-free fax/phone: 1-800-542-4611
www.ElizabethGeorge.com
www.JimGeorge.com

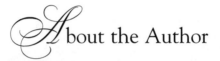

About the Author

Elizabeth George is a bestselling author and speaker whose passion is to teach the Bible in a way that changes women's lives. For information about Elizabeth's books or speaking ministry, to sign up for her mailings, or to share how God has used this book in your life, please write to Elizabeth at:

Elizabeth George
P.O. Box 2879
Belfair, WA 98528

Toll-free fax/phone: 1-800-542-4611
www.ElizabethGeorge.com

∼

God Loves His Precious Children

Jim and Elizabeth George share the comfort of Psalm 23 with children in original prose. Engaging watercolor scenes and memorable rhymes bring the truths of each verse to life and invite young ones to gather God's promises along the way.

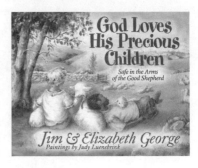

God's Wisdom for Little Girls

Sugar and spice and everything nice—that's what little girls are made of...and so much more! Best-selling author Elizabeth George draws from the wisdom of the book of Proverbs to encourage young girls to apply the positive traits and qualities illustrated in each verse.

Judy Luenebrink's charming illustrations complement the text, which emphasizes that there is more to being a girl than simply being sweet and nice. God desires for them to be helpful, confident, thoughtful, eager, prayerful, creative, cheerful, and kind—one of His little girls!

God's Wisdom for Little Boys

Share with the little boy in your life the gift of God's wisdom from Proverbs, and celebrate with him the character and traits of a godly man. As you read together fun rhymes that illustrate wisdom and strength, he will discover how special he is as a child of God.

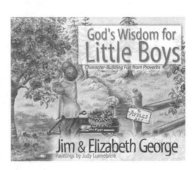

Judy Luenebrink's vibrant illustrations will capture the attention of little boys...and the adults who are reading to them.

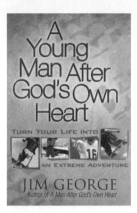

A Young Man After God's Own Heart

Jim George takes teenagers on a radical journey of faith. Through God's extreme wisdom and powerful insights from the life of warrior and leader King David, readers will discover biblical principles that blaze a trail to godly living. *A Young Man After God's Own Heart* helps guys grow into men who honor God in all they do. Great for Sunday school, youth group studies, and individual reading.

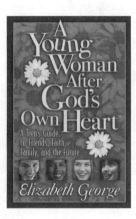

A Young Woman After God's Own Heart

This young woman's version of Elizabeth George's bestselling book *A Woman After God's Own Heart*® shares the intentions and blessings of God's heart with teen girls. On this journey they discover His priorities for their lives—including prayer, submission, faithfulness, and joy—and how to embrace those priorities in daily life.

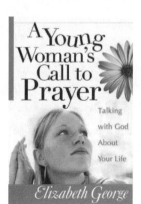

A Young Woman's Call to Prayer

From her own journey, the Bible, and the lives of others, Elizabeth reveals the explosive power and dynamic impact of prayer on everyday life. *A Young Woman's Call to Prayer* gives step-by-step guidance for experiencing an enthusiastic prayer life. Great for Sunday school, group studies, and individual reading.

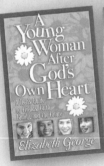

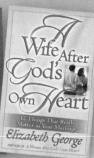

A Woman After God's Own Heart® Study Series

Bible Studies for Busy Women

God wrote the Bible to change hearts and lives. Every study in this series is written with that in mind—and is especially focused on helping Christian women know how God desires for them to live."

—Elizabeth George

Sharing wisdom gleaned from more than 20 years as a women's Bible study teacher, Elizabeth has prepared insightful lessons that can be completed in 15 to 20 minutes per day. Each lesson includes thought-provoking questions, insights, Bible study tips, instructions for leading a discussion group, and a "heart response" section to make the Bible passage more personal.

Living with Passion and Purpose — LUKE — Elizabeth George — 0-7369-0816-1

Becoming a Woman of Beauty & Strength — ESTHER — Elizabeth George — 0-7369-0489-1

Putting On a Gentle & Quiet Spirit — 1 PETER — Elizabeth George — 0-7369-0290-2

Discovering the Treasures of a Godly Woman — PROVERBS 31 — Elizabeth George — 0-7369-0818-8

Nurturing a Heart of Humility — CHARACTER STUDIES MARY — Elizabeth George — 0-7369-0300-3

Walking in God's Promises — CHARACTER STUDIES SARAH — Elizabeth George — 0-7369-0301-1

Experiencing God's Peace — PHILIPPIANS — Elizabeth George — 0-7369-0289-9

Pursuing Godliness — 1 TIMOTHY — Elizabeth George — 0-7369-0665-7

Cultivating a Life of Character — JUDGES/RUTH — Elizabeth George — 0-7369-0498-0

Growing in Wisdom & Faith — JAMES — Elizabeth George — 0-7369-0490-5

HARVEST HOUSE PUBLISHERS
EUGENE, OREGON 97402
www.harvesthousepublishers.com

Books by Elizabeth George

- Beautiful in God's Eyes
- Encouraging Words for a Woman After God's Own Heart®
- God's Wisdom for a Woman's Life
- Life Management for Busy Women
- Loving God with All Your Mind
- A Mom After God's Own Heart
- Powerful Promises for Every Woman
- The Remarkable Women of the Bible
- A Wife After God's Own Heart
- A Woman After God's Own Heart®
- A Woman After God's Own Heart® Deluxe Edition
- A Woman After God's Own Heart® Prayer Journal
- A Woman's Call to Prayer
- A Woman's High Calling
- A Woman's Walk with God
- A Young Woman After God's Own Heart
- A Young Woman's Call to Prayer

Children's Books

- God's Wisdom for Little Girls

Study Guides

- Beautiful in God's Eyes Growth & Study Guide
- God's Wisdom for a Woman's Life Growth & Study Guide
- Life Management for Busy Women Growth & Study Guide
- Loving God with All Your Mind Growth & Study Guide
- A Mom After God's Own Heart Growth & Study Guide
- Powerful Promises for Every Woman Growth & Study Guide
- The Remarkable Women of the Bible Growth & Study Guide
- A Wife After God's Own Heart Growth & Study Guide
- A Woman After God's Own Heart® Growth & Study Guide
- A Woman's Call to Prayer Growth & Study Guide
- A Woman's High Calling Growth & Study Guide
- A Woman's Walk with God Growth & Study Guide

Books by Jim & Elizabeth George

- God Loves His Precious Children
- God's Wisdom for Little Boys
- Powerful Promises for Every Couple
- Powerful Promises for Every Couple Growth & Study Guide

Books by Jim George

- God's Man of Influence
- A Husband After God's Own Heart
- A Man After God's Own Heart
- The Remarkable Prayers of the Bible
- A Young Man After God's Own Heart